The Ten Thousand Things:

My Mother, The Desert, And Life On The Colorado Plateau

Colorado Plateau

UTAH

COLORADO

Zion NP

Mountain Meadow Massacre

Paria Ghost Town

Navajo Res

Kanab

Lake Powell

Colorado River

W

E

Colorado City

The Dam

Navajo Mtn

Lee's Ferry

Home: Page

Four Corners

Grand Canyon

N.Rim

S.Rim

HOPI

Sante Fe

Flagstaff (Grocery Store)

Road to Indiana

Albuquerque

Mama's house (Retirement)

ARIZONA

NEW MEXICO

Not to scale
My home and surroundings
7th Grade Social Studies class

The Ten Thousand Things:

My Mother, The Desert,
And Life On The Colorado Plateau

Debbi Flittner

LIZARD WISDOM PUBLISHING

Portland, Oregon

Lizard Wisdom Publishing
Copyright ©2025 by Debra Flittner

Author's note: This book is based on the author's most accurate recollections of people and experiences over time.

Conversations, especially early ones, have been recreated where memory is imperfect, to reflect the character of individuals as experienced by the author. Timelines of events may be compressed or may not be presented in exact chronological order.

Some names have been changed to honor the privacy of individuals. Some names have been left unchanged to honor the lives of deceased individuals. The author's spiritual experiences are her own.

Published by Lizard Wisdom Publishing

Portland, Oregon

You may reach the author directly at **www.debbiflittner.com.**

ISBN: 979-8-9924242-1-8

ISBN e: 979-8-9924242-0-1

Library of Congress Control: 2025905271

Cover photos by the author

Cover design and interior design by Joanna Wiley

Interior images by the author drawn from photographs or private collection

Pottery images by the author drawn from holdings on display at Verde Valley Archeology Center and Museum

Author photo on back cover: James Hagerman

Lizard Wisdom Publishing in Portland, Oregon is located on the unceded homelands of the:

Atfalati; Kalapuya; Confederated Tribes of Siletz Indians and Confederated Tribes of Grand Ronde.

I give thanks continually for the harsh beauty of the red rock landscape
and the tribal cultures whose ways surrounded me in early life.
Both shaped me.
—And for the feminine lineage, in human and cosmic form, that shows
me daily that life is a sacred journey, and a mystery.
We go on, in love.

I am home in the desert. There are steep canyons
before me carved away by water, by wind. I see an opening in the Earth. I
feel an opening in my heart...

This is my prayer:
to gather together, to speak freely, to question and be questioned, to love
and be loved, to feel the pulse, this seismic pulse—it will guide us beyond
fear.

—Terry Tempest Williams, Red

Contents

Contents (continued)

Contents (continued)

PROLOGUE

The Tao that can be told is not the eternal Tao;
The name that can be named is not the eternal name.
The nameless is the beginning of heaven and earth.
The named is the mother of ten thousand things.
~ Tao Te Ching

How can I make sense of my early life, a time of turmoil that I often feel but don't clearly remember? Trying to recall those years of loneliness and chaos brings up a jumble of feelings, a patchwork of memories. Memories like home movies that jump from scene to scene instead of playing through to the end; there's no sequence or order. There's not a way to slow it down, either. But these memories and feelings need to be slowed down, need to be slowed down and held with love, in order to let them unfold. It's in the unfolding that I face what they still hold, it's how they can in time let go of their raw emotion and become lighter, easier to carry.

I'm feeling now into the spaces of those early years. Breathing in, I exhale and relax a little. This slows things, brings me a step or two back from that intensity of thought. The larger space now sparks a flow, more feeling and sensation than memory—more like a river now—the imprint of the "ten thousand things" of those early years.

A light breeze from an open window moves across my face as I sit on my cushion, flattened from years of use, here in the meditation corner upstairs in my house. In front of me, an old Chinese altar holds a photo of two spiritual teachers. A vase of incense, its purple-blue smoke spiraling upward anchors a corner, while a photo of my daughter and me in front of a Tibetan temple sits at another. Under the windowsill, a shelf holds goddesses; a statue of a black Madonna from Spain, one of Kwan Yin, and another of the Virgin of Guadalupe from New Mexico. All of these are as steadying as my meditation cushion.

Exhaling, I slide forward off the cushion and pull it to me, patting it soundly around the edges to fluff it back in shape. Settling back on, I relax again into my internal world. I close my eyes and again find that nothing is still in this swirling, aware field, except awareness itself—that wide-open gentle space that holds every moment of my life, the everything-ness of it all; inside of me, around me, and far beyond me, too. It holds all in an endless quiet, and softly waits.

I open my eyes, and now they come to rest above me, on a Tibetan thangka painting of Milarepa, a spiritual master and poet. He sits on an animal skin, the Himalayan mountains in the background; his skin faintly green from years of living on nettle tea. His hand cocked to his ear, his body tense, he leans and listens. He listens for the teaching songs of his master; I listen inside to the fading hazy images of long-ago time and space. Behind that inner fog, stronger feelings well up now from some deeper place in my belly. Rising up through my throat, my eyes now glisten with tears—but then—something in me pushes them all away. Again.

How do I coax these feelings that fly toward and then away from me like frightened birds, how do I get them to slow down, circle, and land, so I can simply be with them? There are so many, whole unnamed flocks of them, born across time during years of my childhood. Feelings that so often circle around my mother as well.

My mother: the elusive, unnerving creature who cast a long, narrow shadow across my childhood, across my whole life. A woman who rarely had much to say; a woman who was ignored and abandoned as a child.

One who apologized to my father for giving birth to me, the last girl of four, and who let her two half-grown daughters name me. The mother who raised me from across the house, through the hands of these first and second-born sisters.

I was a girl who wore thick glasses by age ten, and braces by twelve. A bashful child who ran as wild as the wind that brought no rain, who blossomed into a desert orphan.

It's a cool spring morning as I sit, giving up meditation to mull over these memories. Sipping a cup of lukewarm coffee, I glance out the high window. The breeze has become a wind, sending branches of the trees into a dance, this way and that, while brave birds cling to them. A scene outside of me, but one that mirrors the inner one. My strong feelings point to some still-murky years.

I hadn't found the deepest headwaters where the most troubling feelings sprang from. Or I hadn't found them all. I'd survived my childhood, though, and found a place in life. A sturdier place inside me, too, that allowed me to put down roots. Roots that gave me a sense of direction that was hard won from sticking with challenging times. I'd framed and hung a collection of old photos, too, of grandparents and great, great relatives. The somber steadiness of their black and white faces watching over me was a steadying comfort, even if I knew little about them.

Passing decades brought new challenges, but good changes, too. I'd felt a deep ache; a longing for something. I wanted a teacher, I realized; I wanted to follow an ancient, well-trodden path, and look for whatever it felt like was missing. I found a teacher and an ashram; I began a meditation practice and dedicated myself to it, and to the books my teacher had written about it. I followed those practices for years, and it led into the core of my own Being. More years passed, as I studied and practiced Tibetan Buddhism, Zen, and then a tantric form of Advaita Vedanta, an ancient Indian philosophy. Daily life became a dialogue between parts of myself and the world around me that were all cloaked in the same warm, pool of Oneness that I had come to know.

I often had far-seeing visions and dreams where I became as expanded and love-filled as this Oneness. I had slowly come to accept these experiences as gifts along the path of unfoldment.

But the peace I'd found grew shaky when my mother came to mind. The memories were still there, and hard. I was cautious around her; I was a bit afraid of her.

She was ninety years old now, still living alone. An image of her came to mind as I set aside my cold coffee. A tall woman in a plain blue bathrobe, frowning down silently over her two youngest children as they watched cartoons on Saturday morning. How those children felt that dark gaze; looked up, then at each other, and went separately to their rooms, all without a word. What was it in that foreboding silence of hers that caused my chest to tighten, even now? The warming breezy day seemed to have suddenly cooled. I reached over and slid the window shut.

My mother, the woman who created the world that my sisters and I grew up in, was the author of ten thousand silences, all laced with loss or fear, each different from the other. Losses that wove a crooked tapestry, which never safely held my childhood.

And yet, I cared deeply about her.

She'd just been diagnosed with a type of slow-progressing dementia. During a visit three months earlier, she'd struggled to keep up in conversation with me. I was shocked at these changes. I decided

I'd be in touch much more often—in spite of the wall between us—and help her if she'd let me. She'll be going through a lot, I thought, with the struggles that are coming. I want to help her, do whatever I can do, even if it's small. It'll be good for us both, I thought, and being around her more might help these old, childhood aches. I called my sister who lived near her, and who watched over her.

"Yeah, she's going downhill. But she doesn't need you, and she'll think you're interfering," my second sister Donna said. "I call her on my way home from work and go with her to medical appointments. At least she'll let me do that now. I stop by most weekends. The neighbors get her mail, and Aunt Jean takes her to the grocery store sometimes."

"I can at least call her more and listen, I know she's lonely. I can buy her things she'll need."

"She's lonely, alright. I try to talk to her, but it's like talking to a rock. It gets old."

"I'll come down more often, then."

"It won't make any difference."

"She'll know that I'm thinking about her."

"Well, I don't need your help, either. I'm used to managing it alone," she said coolly. We'd had this talk before.

Well, Donna may not need help, but my mother does, I thought.

She's my mother, too.

I. IT BEGINS

CHAPTER 1

Mama: Age Ninety-Two

"She fell again," Donna says on a group telephone call with me and my sister Sandi.

"She got up to go to the bathroom last night, and I guess in the low light, she got confused and fell. She was right by her bed, though, so she called me. I had to drive her to emergency at 2:00 in the morning. Yes, again. I guess I could put more nightlights in there, and then she'll have her own Las Vegas strip to light up the way. There's already one in every wall."

"I'm sorry for that, for both of you," says Sandi. "It just goes on, I know. But I feel for her, being in the hospital again."

"Was she hurt? Can we call her?" I ask.

"Yeah, I just got off the phone with the floor nurse before I called you both. She didn't hit anything, and was on the carpet, so I don't know. She said her back hurt. They'll keep her long enough to do some X-rays and a full checkup today. I vaguely know the nurse I spoke to—she works on the floor above mine. I'll check on her in the morning when I'm back at work," says Donna, a nurse at the hospital where Mama is now in care. "I'll call you back when I hear. But in the meantime, she does have a room, so you can reach her."

"I'll call her now. I bet she'll say she's fine and wants to come home."

I hang up, and speed-dial the hospital's main number. They transfer me to her room.

"Mama? How are you? I heard you took a tumble, and they're looking you over."

"Donna?"

"No, it's Deb."

"Deb?"

"Yeah; how are you? Can you hear me okay?"

"Yes, I hear you fine. I feel alright. My back's a little sore. I hope they let me go home today. I have things I need to get done."

~

"I just heard from the hospital again," Donna says, the next afternoon. "She has a tiny spinal fracture in a vertebra. And apparently, the X-ray shows several other fractures from her past. And, also, she has pneumonia! It gets even better. Her doctor said that she's so weak, and her thinking is off enough that the hospital won't release her to live by herself. She'll need home care, at a minimum. I don't know how we're going to tell her about that one. Or what kind of personal help she'll agree to. So far, none. She just says, 'I don't want strangers in my house.'"

"I don't know either. She'll probably be in the hospital a week or two, though," Sandi says.

"They'll clear up the pneumonia, the fracture will hopefully heal, and then, he said, they'll send her to rehab, so she'll be there awhile, too. I don't know what we'll do after that. We probably have a few weeks to figure it out." Donna falls silent.

"You know that military pension I mentioned?" I sat the phone down, walked over to a desk and picked up a thick manila file. "I've been checking into it, and it's really dense reading, but I think Mama qualifies for it."

"I doubt it," says Donna. "And even if she does, it'll be forever before she gets it."

"Well, there's three of us," I say. "This is my kind of policy stuff. I want to try. It's either that, or we'll need to sell her house, or pay for her care ourselves. The application asks for tons of medical and financial records, but I've figured out what we'll need. Getting it is another thing. I found good instructions for working through it, though. I think it's possible."

"I'll help you, Deb," Sandi says. "Let's try."

Donna is silent again on the other end of the phone. "Well, you two do whatever you want. Let me know how it goes. If you need something, I'll see what I can do. But I don't have the time for it. And I don't like paperwork."

～

"I cannot believe this," Sandi says, four months later. "I just got a call from Pete at the veteran's office, the guy that sent Mama's application in. He says we've gotten approved! And for a full pension award! They're going to give Mama the maximum amount."

"What? You're kidding. When did he call?"

"Just ten minutes before I called you! He sounded surprised. Said he doesn't see a decision in four months very often, and hardly ever for that amount. It was scary spending down what she had after she got out of rehab so she'd qualify, but it worked."

"I still can't believe it."

"I told him about that letter you wrote to the senator, asking for help. He said that moved the dial, because they put people in their nineties ahead of the crowd. The senator's office knew this. They got her to the head of the line! Or at least into the shorter line."

"Sandi, I don't even know what to say," I reply. "Give me a second." Sitting the phone on the counter, I pour a cold glass of water, and take a long drink. Glancing out the kitchen window, I notice the warmth of the day unfolding, as it does every day, moment by moment.

"This changes everything, you know. Although Mama won't grasp what we've pulled off. That's okay, I know. But after months of making calls and reading about what to do, and then gathering records, the application part went pretty fast. Man, I'm so glad you could go down there last fall and chase down those medical records I needed. I couldn't have done that. I doubt Donna would've helped me with that."

"Yeah, that's probably true."

"Let's call her and give her the news!"

"Are you sure? She's in? For the maximum amount?" Donna almost shouts in disbelief. "Well, that is a big game-changer. It truly is. I've got another place to visit, but I like the one I told you about last week. That pension will cover the entire cost. Although it still took forever to get through all that government red tape. What a mess! What a relief to me. Mama won't get it and will be dead-set against moving. She doesn't like the caregivers coming, and it's not enough, anyway. We need them overnight, when she tends to fall. Now we just have to convince her to move before she really hurts herself. I am dreading having that talk. Can I say that again?"

"Yeah, I am, too. That's going to be nothing short of devastating. But there's no way around it. She loves that house. She's been there, what? Close to forty years?"

I nod, agreeing with Sandi. "Maybe forty-five by now," I added. "I think she feels close to Daddy there, even though he's gone. When you do finally bring it up to her, Donna, call us right away. I'll call her as soon as I hear from you. I think that'll help."

"Alright. I just really dread it. I do feel good about that place, though."

CHAPTER 2

Chimayo: A Backroad Into Memory

Brightest New Mexico. In the vivid light each rock and tree and cloud and mountain existed with a kind of force and clarity that seemed not natural but supernatural. Yet it also felt as familiar as home, the country of dreams, the land I had known from the beginning.
~ Edward Abbey

Pulling the rental car into the sandy driveway by the casita, I exhale. I'm here, finally, after the long drive north from the Albuquerque airport. Alone with the quiet space I've needed for months. I've come back to the state I made my home at twenty-four, the place that claimed my heart. The place I moved to after a teenage marriage and a painful divorce; where I found comfort in the land and people. The place where I raised my daughter, born during my last teenage year. Growing up beside her in a land that held us both, I came to love this warm enchanted place that took me in, that let me claim it; that marked me as one of its own and helped me make a life here.

I've come back now for solace, for the peace offered by this casita and the Santuario de Chimayo, an old pilgrimage site in the nearby village. Rolling my suitcase to the door, I look around the property I've rented for the next eight days. An acre-size pond sits out front, with cattails and grasses that surround smooth, blue water. A few ducks swim about, quacking softly and diving for food. Hummingbirds whiz back and forth from a feeder. Cottonwood trees circle the pond, their branches waving with the gentle breeze. Further out past the cottonwoods, small bronze hills dotted with juniper and cedar keep watch. Quiet surrounds me here. I breathe a sigh—it's good to feel at home again, here in a desert oasis—and turn the key in the door and step inside the casita.

The three years since Mama's dementia diagnosis have been surreal, heightening from dreamlike haze to a steely hardness over the last few weeks. Almost imperceptibly, Mama's health has declined even further. At ninety-four years old, her legs gave out three weeks ago, surprising the caregiver walking her to breakfast. He caught her and sat her in a wheelchair. She hasn't stood on her own or walked since then.

We don't speak of it, my sisters and I carry our mother's silence, but it is a sign. A cloud of pain, a numbness hovers over her, spreading out across time and space, drawing me and my sisters in from three different states. Her mother-pull is darkly strong, and each new decline takes her further away from us, highlighting our helplessness to stop it. Her unhappiness, her half-spoken demands that we somehow shift the course of her life, add to the whispering silence. I could have spent these eight days visiting her, but I've chosen not to. I'd leave more exhausted than when I got there, I tell myself, and she wouldn't be glad to see me, either. She'd been this way all my life, but her age and illness make things worse now. I couldn't decide the best thing to do when my meditation retreat was canceled, and I found myself with an open week. I tried to make myself buy a plane ticket to go see her in Arizona. I loved the area and could hike when I needed a break from her. But I came here, instead.

This downward spiral in her health is tiring. Everything from how her room is arranged, the clothes she can wear, her medication dosages, has to be reviewed and changed with her caretakers, with everyone aware of what's happening. The group phone calls with my two sisters go on too long. With my oldest sister gone— the one who ran the household when our mother was too tired—my mother's plan to someday live with her evaporated.

Gone eight years now, from a life of poor health made worse by drugs and alcohol, we three who remain struggle to fill the gap she left in our mother's life. We talk around the subject of a mother we've never really known, who has become angry as she's fed or bathed; who is slipping away. The sister who lives near her house seems oblivious, still thinking she'll improve if only this or that is changed; the other frets constantly, talking about little else besides this slow, agonizing descent. The back-and-forth talks mask what's really happening.

But there will be rest here, with limited cell service at the casita. If she suddenly dies, they'll reach me somehow, I think, in my worn-out state. Or figure out what to do without me.

I unpack. I spend slow, sweet time arranging groceries for the week ahead, in the refrigerator and on the tile countertop, placing fruit and ripening avocados in a pretty blue bowl that I find. The adobe fireplace, with its wildly shaped cottonwood angels hovering nearby, comforts me. The warm, terracotta tile floor invites bare feet, and I slip shoes off and pour myself a glass of wine. Stepping outside and settling onto the wooden bench under the portal, I watch hummingbirds feed near a garden statue of Saint Francis. Tall sunflowers by the pond sway in the early autumn breeze. My thoughts turn again, unbidden, to my mother. She would like it here.

Memories flood in, as if the wine loosened the knots of time. I recall better times with my mother. How I'd drive over from Albuquerque to see her for the weekend, and how she'd be waiting outside for my daughter and me, sitting on the bench in the carport, listening for my car wheels on the quiet, rural road. How she'd jump up as I shut the car off, her dark, unreadable face breaking into a wide smile, how I'd peel myself out of the car after that long drive, ready to hug her. She'd come toward me, her long stride bringing her quickly to the car, hesitating enough to remind me how awkward and uncomfortable she was hugging anyone. We'd move toward each other and, hugging her lightly, I'd wait to feel a hug back, a hug that would come as she lightly tapped my shoulders, pressed her hands slightly into them, laughed uncomfortably, and stepped back. The familiar scent of her soap and sweat and hairspray filled my nose. We'd gather our luggage and follow her, my daughter chatting about school, or what we saw along the way; Mama answering with a hmm or an uh-huh; me eager to hear her stories of what she'd been doing.

"Come in! I've got some cold sun tea I made for you both just this morning," she'd say, "and I made a new enchilada recipe for dinner. Take your things on into the spare bedroom."

Still smiling, she might say, "Did you notice my new hair-do? I had them add some color this time, since it's gotten so white," or "Come see the new rosebush I just had planted outside." I'd follow, grateful for her animation, wanting to keep it going, wanting to hear about everything. Wanting to share everything.

But by the next day, toward the afternoon or evening, her conversation would slow and then stop. She'd retreat to her recliner in front of the always-on television and have little more to say.

Still, I loved those visits, I thought, walking slowly into the casita, pulling a ready-made dinner from the refrigerator. I miss them. We were glad to see each other, at least at first, and it was pretty there; the sort of desert oasis I loved. I missed her already, I realized.

~

After a long night's sleep and a morning cup of coffee out on the portal, I drive into the village of Chimayo and pull up in the dusty parking lot next to the old, sacred church of the same name, Santuario de Chimayo. Grief wells up through layers of numbness around my mother's life. She hates the assisted living place we found for her, after she was hospitalized again for pneumonia. Falling too often while living alone, her doctors said she wasn't safe at her house, no matter how much she insisted she was. She asked to go home for months, and I cried every time she said that, knowing what she didn't—she wouldn't live there ever again; the house she'd lived in for forty years. Decades of sitting on her patio bench watching the flaming desert sunsets were over for us both. She must have surely sensed this.

The house was small; a tan adobe-type brick house that she and my father spent years building for when they retired, moving there while I was still a teenager. The house where she and my father lived together only five years before his sudden death from a heart attack. A death that was fast and shocking for a healthy man of sixty-four, and for the wife he left behind. But she'd gotten through it, had rallied, found a sort of freedom she'd never really had before. Living alone for thirty-five more years there was a long time. After two years in an assisted living home, she was very frail. And with dementia, she was in a precarious state.

I leave the car and walk slowly into the chapel, feeling the warm, adobe walls reach out and wrap around me. I take in the living compassion they softly emanate. Further into the Santuario I settle onto a worn, wooden pew. Tears fall, and I let them; tears for the mother who couldn't wrap her arms around me, couldn't reach out that way, like the walls of the chapel had done. I remember that broken place in her, how it held her back, when what I wanted so badly was a mother whose love was certain. The tears slow, so I walk to the front of the vestibule to light a candle for her. I think of the times we never had, and the slight hold she now has on life.

"For you, Mama," I silently say, placing the candle down with the others. "For you, mother of all those ten thousand messy things. May this candle help you find your way."

I imagine it sending her a stream of pure love. Comforting the woman I know, the one I longed for, and the one it's too late to know.

The heart of the Santuario draws me further, into the room where pilgrims have gathered over time, rubbing themselves with holy sand believed to have healing properties. I bend down and take some into my hands. Feeling the warm graininess, I rub it between my palms, letting it flow through my fingers. I lift my hands to my neck and face, rubbing the gritty warmth into my skin, soaking in what it offers. The voices of people who have grieved and found comfort here for centuries whisper softly. I pause to see where all four walls are lined with crutches, glasses, and canes, left behind by those who walked out on their own. The sight of this lightens my spirit.

~

I drive into Chimayo each day, repeating these quiet tasks, and light a fresh candle to hold the waning life of my mother. I return after to the casita and rest and watch the pond, thinking of those years here in New Mexico, how impossibly hard it had all been at first—deciding that I, a single mom, would go to college and then law school—the first person in my family to go into higher education. There had been no money to fund this idea. Remembering the cozy apartment my daughter and I had near the university in the "student ghetto," where snippets of mariachi or classical music was always in the air, where someone might be crossing the street singing an opera; where the smell of green chile wafted out of the plentiful, cheap restaurants lining the street. Recalling how I slept on the couch for years, giving the only bedroom to my daughter. How I'd pick her up each afternoon at the nearby elementary school. We'd sometimes go for a drive and find ourselves down by the Rio Grande, or up on cliffs at a spot overlooking the city, sitting on the car hood, watching the sunset light up the building windows and the Sandia Mountains behind them. How my daughter's life in school, and mine in college, echoed each other; full of teachers and friends and professors; how I was surprised to find academics so easy, and that I loved it. It all seemed clear, the singular direction we both should go, back then.

A chill in the evening air brings me back to the quiet of the pond. Drawing a shawl around my shoulders, I lift myself off the deep chair under the portal, and soon enough find myself tossing and turning in the bed.

At week's end, I spend the evening gathering up clothes and the few things I've purchased here. I set aside the three small hand-carved cottonwood angels I bought in the Santuario gift shop. I'll carry these home in my hands. In the morning I zip up my luggage and drag it out under the portal, pausing for a last look at the pond. I say a goodbye to the casita, and it glows warmly back at me. With my bags in the car, I wave to Saint Francis and the hummingbirds, then roll slowly up the dirt road to the highway, clouds of dust fanning out behind the car wheels. On the freeway I turn south, toward Albuquerque, toward my distant Pacific Northwest home.

CHAPTER 3

The Dark: A Family

I'm three years old. I'm lying in a big tent. It's black all around, dark trees are everywhere. We're camping in our tent. It's snuggly. My sisters and parents are sleeping around me. Then I hear a sound.

Blackness surrounds me, and I'm alone with the sound.

Mama? Mama!

Wailing, screaming tremors come from outside, somewhere in the dark beyond our tent.

It's louder, closer, and now it's everywhere around me—inside and outside the tent—it's coming from everything.

Sounds come from me now, and I'm screaming too. Everything, everywhere is screaming.

Is the fear inside or outside of me?

I'm scared!

Mama? Mama!

There's no one there. Sobs wracking my belly, I cry and cry, and then remember nothing more.

The next morning: shuffling around a hot campfire, long metal stick in my hand, holding marshmallows over a flame and watching them glow red and catch fire; my face smeared and sticky with earlier successes.

~

For too many years, this memory haunts me. Tent and darkness and wild, inhuman sounds. Monsters in a nightmare, I decide.

I'm in my twenties, sitting at the scratched-up oak table on my mother's porch; my three sisters and I have gathered there. Our lives have grown far apart, but our mother's birthday still brings us back to her house in the desert.

"I remember camping in the big dark green army tent. It was huge, so we all fit in it. We'd go camping along riverbanks or in a meadow by the woods, especially in the summer and fall. Sheep woke us up once," first sister Lynn says. "Was I there?" I ask, as small thoughts join together and become a picture faintly painting itself alive.

"Yes, you were really little, but you were there."

"I remember screaming in that tent in the dark. I was terrified! I thought I had a nightmare about monsters."

"Oh no, no," she says, throwing her head back and laughing, drinking down her glass of wine. "It wasn't a nightmare or monsters at all. It happened. But it was Basque shepherds. They were moving a huge flock of sheep, and came right through our camp. The sheep were bleating; it made a huge ruckus. It was dark, but probably early dawn. We couldn't even hear each other in the tent over the noise. I doubt if Mama even heard you." She paused, refilling her wine glass almost to the brim. "But you know Mama. She missed a lot on a good day."

Shaken by this new story and her laughter at my childish terror, I scoot my chair away from hers and watch her lift her glass again, remembering. *I've always been afraid of you.*

The old fear reverberates across dark time through my belly, still full of that living energy of the past.

And the taste of campfire marshmallows.

CHAPTER 4

Sisters

Oh, my sisters.

First sister Lynn has wolf eyes. She hides far away, in the distance, where I can't see her. She watches me from there, waiting for me to stumble. I don't really know her, she goes to high school all day. I'm four. If she's home, I better watch out.

"Ouch, wah!—Mama!" I cry, grabbing a chair arm to pull myself up off the living room floor. My chin burns, and I touch it and find something slippery and wet. It's running down my neck.

"You're mean! You tripped me!" Screaming, I run into the kitchen for Mama, wiping more blood onto my shirt.

"What now?" Mama says with a glare, turning away from a steaming pot on the stove. Wiping her hands on a dishtowel, she sighs as I run to hide behind her. But Lynn cuts in between Mama and me. I look around her at Mama.

"Something's wrong with her, Mama," she says. "She has big feet. She tripped over them and fell on her face, right in front of me."

She glowers down at me, but Mama hesitates, glancing over toward her pot.

Breathing in ragged sobs, I open my mouth to protest, but my words won't come out. *I'm scared of her. That's not what happened!*

Frowning, Mama looks over at Lynn. "Go get her a washcloth and a band-aid. And get her a clean shirt. Go. Now!"

"And you, let your sister change your shirt. Then go play in your room. I don't have time for this!" Mama turns back to her cook pot.

My sister comes back, carrying only a shirt. She doesn't bring a washcloth or any Band-Aids. She smirks sideways eyes at me.

Wolf eyes.

~

"Okay! I'm leaving for the store. I'll be gone awhile. Mind your big sister while I'm out."

That sister, the mean one, looks across the room at me as Mama talks, her eyes like slits. She smiles thinly at me, her lips tight. My heart racing, I run to third sister Sandi who is barely older than me. We turn and walk toward the hallway as Mama slams the door. Walking on our toes in sock feet down the dark hallway, we make it to the bedroom door. It doesn't squeak as I close it behind us. It's a good door.

But there's no lock.

Maybe she'll forget about us. Sometimes she does.

She stole my baby last time Mama left, my Casper the Friendly Ghost. He was missing off my bed, and wasn't in my doll crib, either.

"Casper!" I screamed, looking through toys in the closet. "Casper, where are you?"

"I hear a bratty baby crying! She's going to get it!" Lynn said, bursting into my room.

I stand there, wide-eyed, looking in her dark eyes, not knowing what to do. A moment passes. I sit down at the closet's edge, with my back to the wall, my eyes on her face.

She steps toward me. "Stop sniffing, big baby, or you'll never get him back!"

But I can't stop.

"Aahh!" I scream as she yanks me up from the floor and shoves me onto my bed. She stands over me, covering my mouth and nose with her hand—her voice a loud whisper, "If you tell Mama when she gets back, I'll crack his head open! Shut up!"

I can't breathe.

I don't remember what happened to Casper, I don't know when Mama got home.

But I remember looking up at her from the bed—her face red and twisted, her eyes black and angry through her glasses.

Mama never comes.

~

My second sister Donna isn't like this. She lets me come into her bedroom.

"Do you want to try some makeup? Can I put this on your eyes?" I nod yes, and she opens a jar, smiling, reaching into it with her pinky. She finger-paints it on me, and then dabs it on her eyes. Then she picks up a tube and twists it open.

"This one goes on lips. It's really red! Would you like some on your lips?" I nod again, and she slides a reddish crayon across my lower and upper lip.

"Okay, now smack your lips together. Oh, it's so bright on you! Do you want to see what you look like?" Nodding, I lean around her and see myself in her big round dresser mirror. My lips glow bright red. I sit watching the two of us in the mirror while she unwinds huge pink foam curlers out of her hair, dropping them one by one on the dresser. Then she brushes her hair.

"Here, you can wear my bracelet, but just for now." It jingles as she snaps it on my wrist. I shake my wrist, and it tinkles like music.

"Okay, I have to get ready now. You can stay a minute, but I have to go soon."

I sit on the bed, watching. She brushes and brushes her hair, turning her head upside down and sideways. She sits up, and it falls into a puffy, tall hairdo. Reaching for a spray can, she aims it toward her head.

"Okay, lean back or I'll spray you, too."

I like it when she's home when Mama is gone, sometimes I'm not so scared. But Lynn yells at her, too. Sometimes they talk about school and boys, though, and laugh together.

My third sister Sandi is my friend, but she's not my twin. She's not!

"Oh, aren't your twins cute," says the store lady to Mama. My sister stands in front of a mirror, trying on a sweater for a school picture. I look in the mirror at the store lady and stick my tongue out at her. But she's talking to Mama. "They're darling in their little checkered dresses." Mama laughs out loud and says, "Well, they're not twins, but almost." Mama points to my sister. "She's seventeen months older, but they look almost the same size, don't they? They do look just like twins when they're dressed alike."

I hate it when Mama dresses us alike. And sometimes she calls me Sandi, and sometimes she calls Sandi my name. She forgets who we are.

Sandi and I have a bedroom together. I like her, but she doesn't say much, and doesn't want to play with me very much. She hides in the closet, even when our mean sister isn't yelling. She hides from everyone. We fight sometimes, too.

"Give me the bubbles! It's my turn," I say.

"No! I had them first," she says. Grabbing her hand, I bite it, hard. Snatching the bubbles away, I drop them, spilling them onto the bedroom rug.

"Mama!" She runs, crying, to find her. I hide

behind our bedroom door, but Mama sends Lynn to find me. Pulling me from the door where I hang on with fingertips, she swats me hard across the back of my head. I glance and see Sandi come back and climb into the closet. Screaming, I break away and run toward her and the closet, but Lynn catches me, hitting me again, laughing at me. She turns and leaves, closing the door.

"Get in, before she comes back," Sandi says. I pull my blankie off my bed, and settle in next to her, covering both of us up. We sit together, crying.

Mama!

Mama never comes.

CHAPTER 5

The Man With Black Glasses

"Your sister's coming home. Why don't you go run up the hill and meet her bus," Mama says, turning back to the television. A man with black glasses has come on with a special report. Mama sits frowning in her blue bathrobe, watching from the couch.

I ran outside so fast I forgot my gloves. I breathe warm air on my cold hands and jump from one foot to the other. The bus pulls up, brakes squealing, and rolls to a stop. Kids pour out the doors. Wide-eyed, Sandi gets off, glances at me, and runs on by. I race to catch up.

"Hey, wait! Why did the bus come early?"

"They let school out. The President got shot! You know, the President of our whole country?" I nod at such a big word. I don't go to school yet, though. But a man got shot with a gun. We run together to our house and fly through the front door. Sandi rushes to Mama, who sits on the couch with my two older sisters, who came home while I was waiting for Sandi. The high school got out early, too. With the television turned up high, the three of them sit silently. Lynn the wolf has an arm wrapped around Mama's shoulder. Donna just sits there, staring. I look sideways at Lynn, but she doesn't look back. Her eyes, too, are on the television.

"Ha," I laugh, because they're so quiet and still. I don't get it. Maybe the television man is making a joke. They don't hear me, don't turn to see me laughing. Now I see Mama's face—still and almost white—as she sits between my sisters. They sit there, like three statues.

"I can't believe this! What the hell!" We jump and turn as Daddy walks in, home early too. He crosses the room in big, fast steps, and squeezes in next to Mama, her face still frozen, watching the man on the television. The couch is full, so Sandi leans on the couch arm next to Daddy, while I sit on the floor next to her.

The newsman looks sternly out from the square television box, talking through his big mustache and black glasses. He talks slowly, says his words one by one. His black tie hangs down the front of his white shirt.

"It is now confirmed that the President of the United States has died at one p.m. Central Standard Time," he says, soberly.

Sandi bursts into loud wails, so I cry, too, reaching over to hug her, even though I don't know the President man. But he got shot. And I don't like it when Sandi cries.

I run to my bedroom and come back with Casper, and hug my sister with one arm, and Casper with the other. We sit on the couch, our faces wet, watching the television. I put my head on Sandi's shoulder, and she puts her arm around my neck. We stay like that for a

long time.

CHAPTER 6

Shattered

Our white house is in a forest of big, dark trees. A single gravel road out front goes up the hill to a highway, where the school bus stops. When it's a warmer afternoon, I walk to the top of the hill and meet Sandi there. She's in first grade and rides the bus for an hour to school every day.

I'm at the hill today as Sandi gets off the bus carrying her metal lunch box. She takes her coat off and ties it around her waist, and we run down the hill laughing, our arms stretched out, our long hair flying.

There are no wolves today.

I was waiting for her bus once, and I heard wolves howling. With my feet stuck to the sidewalk, I listened as that high, wavering sound came again. Then I turned and ran home as a sick, cold feeling grew in my stomach. Breathing hard, I opened and slammed the front door behind me and ran upstairs to my room, too scared to look around in case there was a pack of them snapping at my feet.

But that was before Sandi got hurt.

She left when that happened, then you sent me away, Mama. And you left, too. I had to go stay at a neighbor's house. At the house with the lady who wore a baseball cap that covered her whole face, and who had a big gash for a mouth.

"We have to go to Sally's now, so I can see your sister, " you say. "Come on."

"No! I don't like her! I don't want to go! I want to see Sandi, too!"

I start screaming as you pick me up—without telling me when you'll be back—and carry me out the front door and across the gravel road to her house. She opens her door and you nod to her, setting me down, still screaming, and turn around and close the door behind you.

I run to the window and watch as you pull your coat in tighter against the cold air. You glance back toward Sally's house, then cross the street and get into the car where Daddy sits waiting behind the steering wheel. Plumes of smoke rise from the exhaust pipe. He backs the car out of the driveway, crunching gravel as I scream, waving to you through the window.

You come and go, Mama, and sometimes you go but don't come back, and I wake up in the morning at Sally's house. I don't know if you'll come for me. Will I see Sandi again? I want to see her but you say she's too sick and I'm too little.

The lady with the baseball cap and frowning face tells you that I cry all day, and it's true.

Sandi fell really hard and got hurt. She fell all the way down the basement stairs and hit her head on the gray concrete floor. I was close by, but didn't hear a sound. It was a warmer winter day, and Mama said we could ride our tricycles outside. They were down in the basement because it was freezing outside, so we'd race them down there, 'round and 'round the pole, peddling hard, chasing in circles until we fell over, shrieking and dizzy.

But I wasn't there when she fell. I was outside the back door, waiting. She was bringing up our tricycles, my strong, six-year-old sister, one set of handlebars over each arm, struggling up each step all by herself.

Daddy was at work, and Mama was resting on her bed.

Maybe Sandi couldn't hold onto the rail.

Maybe she called for me and I didn't hear her.

No one told her not to bring them both up.

I'm outside, my coat zipped up high against the cold air and blue winter sky, with mittens that are fuzzy inside, and my red scarf on too. I'm waiting and waiting and my sister doesn't come. I'm waiting by the back door to the kitchen, right outside where the steps go down to the basement.

Did I wonder where she was? Did I go see what was taking her so long? What would you have done if you were five, Mama?

I don't really remember what happened. But it must have been like this: tired of waiting, I open the back door, step inside, and look down into the dimly lit basement. I can't see anything. I look over and turn the light switch on. Faint light shines on my sister, crumpled up in a pile at the bottom of the stairs. My tricycle is across her back legs. I go down and look at her. Drops of blood trickle out of her ear. I yell her name and she shakes but doesn't open her eyes.

What came after: memory blinks on, and I'm screaming in the kitchen. No one's there; the kitchen counters are high, the blue sky is high above them outside the window. The square tile on the kitchen floor shines black here, white there—a checkerboard. Wild with fear, I scream and scream for help, for someone to come. No one comes. Memory blinks off.

And next, I remember: I'm at Sally's house, Mama, where you leave me, crying, hands steaming up the cold glass. You get into a car with Daddy. My whole family is gone—days and nights for weeks—I still don't know why.

~

One night, a long time after Sandi fell, I listen at your bedroom door when you and Daddy talk and I learn much more: my sister fell so hard that morning, that the bare basement concrete fractured her skull over her left ear. She fell unconscious and did not respond when spoken to. She was shaking when she was laid on a blanket in the backseat of the family car and taken into town to the hospital, where she was in a coma for weeks.

Twice her heart stopped beating. Twice the doctors were able to restart it.

Daddy said the doctors told them she was very

lucky to be alive after a fall like that, but she wouldn't make it through another one.

"You've got to watch those girls closer. They were alone, trying to get those trikes up."

"I was tired, and laid down for a few minutes."

Mama is tired a lot. She lays down on her bed after Daddy leaves, and stays a long time.

I'm still five when my sister comes back home. I don't know how long she was gone, or when she came back. One day, she was just there. I don't even remember that day.

Mama, did I go with you to the hospital to get her?

Could she walk in the door by herself?

Was she glad to be home?

Did I hug her?

The fear and loneliness must surely have come to an end.

~

It took many years for me to recognize that this wasn't a single event, but an entire series: my sister was injured and almost died. She was in the hospital, in the town an hour from our house, for a long time. And after that night, the whole family left as suddenly as that accident, and didn't return together. I saw Mama on some days, when she left the hospital and drove home briefly to see me. The rest of the family trickled in much later; a sister here, Daddy there.

Lynn came home from somewhere, maybe staying with friends near the hospital, then Donna arrived home from somewhere else, probably in town. Then Daddy appeared.

Nobody said much about the accident. Mama said nothing at all, not even where she and Daddy had been staying in town.

So many kinds of silence.

No one asked if I missed Sandi, or where I was for those missing weeks or months—when my sister was a living ghost, and I was another kind of ghost.

But something inside the young child I was got crushed too, and struggled to come back, to be whole. The wolves were still out there, and inside me now, as well. Life couldn't be the same, because our family had also been shattered by the accident. The reassembly afterward had not, for me, taken hold.

At five years old, I couldn't be sure it wouldn't happen again.

III. DESCENT

CHAPTER 7

The Return

Shaking off memories as the airport loudspeaker blares, I stop to pick up my luggage at baggage claim, and make my way outside into the cool, misty evening. I find a waiting shuttle to the car parking lot, and take a seat inside. The plight of my mother and our chaotic early life still grip me, and I think I've missed my stop until I see it just ahead. Stepping off into the dimming evening, a few people appear out of the fog, huddled together at the stop—a small crowd of hazy shadows, their shape outlined by the streetlight behind them.

Startled, I stop and stare. Yes. That old memory. The one before this lifetime.

~

There is stillness, a haze and softness filtering through and around me. A "me" is aware and perceives this, that the haze is a part of me. I don't know how I see the haze and softness. It flows all around, yet there is a solid awareness in this haze, a dot that is "me" having thoughts.

Three towering beings flow within the haze, forming an arc around the filmy essence that is me. In some way of knowing, they are familiar; thought flows between us without bodies. No words are spoken out loud, but words are heard all the same.

I'm hearing that I have to go. I am replying that I don't want to. A sense of vast pressure flows throughout the filmy softness; there is also an awareness among the beings that at one time I had wanted to go.

The largest being silently says yes, you must. The others, though silent, say they agree. The cycle of descent has begun, they wordlessly say. It has started.

I don't want to go. I sense it will be very hard, embracing this particular life.

Then, a deeper haze covers all; I remember nothing more.

~

Standing in the bus stop shelter, I take a breath, remembering where I am now, and look around for my car. I finally spot it and walk there, my luggage rolling along behind me, this secret ancient memory tingling alive through my body. A memory rooted inside me from somewhere else across time. It's clung to me, never fading— this memory of the three beings, shepherding me forward. I think of the warm casita I just left in New Mexico, wondering at the significance of the three cottonwood angels I've carried back. I pull into my driveway, having somehow driven from the airport to my Pacific Northwest home.

I'm sitting on my couch eating a warmed-through dinner, when I find a voice message from Sandi. Sitting my dinner plate down, I put my phone on speaker and listen.

"Hey, I just heard this. I know you're just getting home, but Mama has lost twenty pounds in two weeks! I can't believe no one told me. Call me back as soon as you can," says my often silent sister, her voice cracking.

I reach her right away.

"I spoke to a nurse this morning at Mama's assisted living place, and she was surprised I didn't know about her weight loss," Sandi says. "I'm so upset. I guess they told Donna yesterday, but she hasn't said anything."

Just two weeks earlier, we signed Mama up for hospice care, after talking with her doctors. She couldn't know, with dementia having dulled her understanding, that we'd made this change. But this latest decline came so quickly, I felt she must have sensed something; maybe felt a kind of permission to start letting go. *Maybe Donna wasn't ready for that*, I thought.

"Do you want me to talk to them about, you know, where she's at?"

"Would you? I don't think I can take more right now, but I want to know."

"It's so late. I'll call them first thing in the morning, then."

I sit my cold dinner down and wheel my suitcase into the bedroom, lifting it up onto the bed. Zipping it open, I toss out dirty clothes and leave in things I may now need to take with me to Arizona. I add more clean clothes, and snacks to eat.

Panicked now about my mother's health, I toss and turn all night, waiting to call the home to see what they can tell us.

I reach them, and they say: *she probably has a week at most to live. I'd come now, if you want to see her.*

I do want to see her.

Hanging up, I call Sandi back. She wants to see her, too.

From two different states, we book flights that arrive close together, at the Arizona airport near our mother. We'll meet there and drive up to her care home together.

I'll be leaving home again in thirty-six hours.

Years ago, I worked with people who only had a short time to live. I loved the honesty of that work. But this is so different—it's my own mother. I watch myself float through the few remaining hours, feet barely touching the ground, as I think about what to take with me that might offer comfort. Remembering her love of big band music, I download files for Glenn Miller, Count Basie, and Ella Fitzgerald onto my phone, and put my WI-FI speaker in my bag. I add harp music, remembering a musician I knew who played for those who were dying. I pick out childhood books to read to her and settle on *The Wizard of Oz* and *Black Beauty*. I slip these into my bag.

I want to bring her something more. I don't know what it could possibly be. I've felt this way for so long,

I realize. Not knowing what to give her, but wanting to make things better for her somehow.

This lifelong effort to bring my mother some rare gift to brighten her day runs deep. The thought circling the edge of my knowing whispers that this is the last chance I'll have.

I'm ready for whatever's next, I decide, or maybe I'm not. I don't know how to be more ready.

I fill my watering can at the sink, and soak my dry houseplants. I sort my mail and catch up in my office until it's time to retrace my steps back to the airport.

~

I check my bag again, and walk through security to my new flight gate.

I startle awake suddenly as the plane bumps around in the hot desert sky, and finally lands. At baggage claim, Sandi spots me lifting my suitcase off the luggage carousel.

"There you are! Oh, man. I know you just got home. I was planning a weekend hike myself, but I knew this was coming soon. I was trying not to schedule anything. God, I'm so glad we're here together."

With tears in my eyes, I nod, not knowing what to say, as I hug her. I'm the silent sister now.

Shrugging off my jacket in the heat, Sandi and I pick up a rental car, and drive north on the freeway, out of the city. Familiar towns and old cafes whiz by. I think of how often I've driven this route for forty years. My sister watches peeling billboards and hills of tall saguaro cactus flash by beneath a hazy blue and orange afternoon sky. Our unspoken words to each other signal the same thought: we're at a juncture we knew was coming, a raw unknown place, deep and wide—a place moving toward us, as we drive to meet it.

The three beings that spoke to me before time fill my mind with their steady presence. A presence that says: *it was foretold that this life would have agonizing hardships. Yet it is your task, and we are watching over you, always.* This brings me comfort. My breath slows; my thoughts settle around what is to come.

I'm about to face a mother I've never been able to fathom, who rarely touched me, and who is now dying. The layers of family history rise to the surface, leaving me helpless, driving north into something I can't retreat from, can't slow down. I hold the steering wheel tight and take slow, long breaths.

We drive until we're hungry, and, spotting a Mexican restaurant, pull off the road. We order take-out, then duck into the general store next door, and buy ready-made sandwiches and some apples to drop off at Mama's house, where we'll stay. At the check-out counter I notice a display of candles and pick one with an image of the Virgin of Guadalupe on it. Eating in the parking lot, we silently crunch tacos filled with spicy meat and salsa. The smell wafts up through the car, through all our tiredness as I pull back onto the freeway.

"We'll be there in another hour, I think. We can swing by Mama's house and drop off our luggage and supplies. It won't take long."

My sister nods, lost in thought.

Soon enough, we pull into the house carport long enough to put our food in the refrigerator and drop off our suitcases. I pull the candle out of the grocery bag and decide to light it now. Mama's kitchen is as tidy and organized as ever, and I find matches easily in a utility drawer. The match sizzles alive, and I touch it to the candle wick. Placing the candle on the sandstone fireplace hearth, I step back and pause, seeing the photos of family sitting above it, on the mantle. Mama's house has stood empty for two years now, but seems brightened by the candle, by our presence here. We lock up briskly, and find the hilly road to the assisted living home a short way from here.

Thoughts of my mother light up the sky of my mind in turbulent, moody colors, as this time, my sister drives on.

CHAPTER 8

Summer Desert Rain

I keep looking over my shoulder in our new house, looking for Lynn, thinking she's after me, forgetting she didn't move here with us. I glance in Donna's bedroom that Lynn would have shared with her, but she isn't here. It's just Donna's room, and it's quiet.

We've moved far south, from the cold, dark forest to the warm desert—I'm almost six years old. Lynn the wolf stayed behind at a friend's house to finish her last year of high school. I don't miss her, ever. I hope she never comes back.

Sandi never says a word about her.

Daddy works for the same government agency that he did in the forest. He helps to build dams that make lakes. We left our old house behind, in the dark woods by an even darker lake. Our new town borders the Navajo Reservation, where Native People live. Most kids in my school live on the reservation, or, like me, they live in town and their parents work for the government.

Our new government house in our desert town is

blue with white trim, and shaped like a rectangle. Every house on the street looks the same, except for the outside, where it's painted a different color.

Mama has a friend named Grace who lives next door in a gray house. Every morning, Mama makes a pot of Folger's coffee, and Grace comes over. With the kitchen smelling like Folger's, Mama and Grace sit talking, drinking coffee, and smoking True Blue cigarettes.

I'm sitting on the couch, coloring a picture of a talking horse who's a sheriff, and listening to Mama and Grace. I listen like a lizard. Lizards hold so still that no one can see them, even though they're sitting right there.

One morning, Mama is smoking and talking at the kitchen table, and then Grace says, "It's such a funny name—'soft drink.'"

"Yes, it is, isn't it? I don't think the girls would even know what it meant. "

"Why don't you ask and see?" Grace said.

Nodding, Mama calls to me: "would you like a soft drink?"

"Oh, yeah!" I say, looking up from coloring, sensing a trick. Setting my coloring book down, I come over, waiting, but Mama looks at Grace, and they both laugh.

"Well, we don't have any," she says, picking up a half-smoked cigarette, red lipstick smudged on one end. She turns back to Grace.

I stand there, waiting for something else, something better from Mama. But instead she laughs and talks on, the haze from her cigarette drifting upward, filling the room. Deflated, I wander off, past the couch where my coloring book still lays.

I open and close the front door softly behind me, noticing the sky had changed. It's early summer; desert monsoon season. Dark, angry clouds now fill the sky overhead. Thunder echoes across and back from distant cliffs and mesas. When Grace first came over, the sky had been sunny.

As I watch, large, slow drops of rain begin to fall. Suddenly, I have an idea—I'll cover myself up with something, make a fort of some kind, and stay outside for the whole storm. Running barefoot to the garage, I grab a big piece of clear plastic, and run back to the driveway, already blotched with rain. Dropping to my knees, I toss the plastic over my head, pulling it tight around me, and tuck it under my feet. The raindrops come down, their loud splatter smacking the plastic faster and faster. It's blurry, but I can see out. I bet no one can see in. I'm invisible.

I stay there, looking through my plastic bubble world, rain pouring down, the sky alive, flashing angry streaks of lightning and cracks of thunder. Water leaks under my toes, but my body is dry.

It's cozy in my little rain-cave. I hum to myself, shrieking with each new clap of thunder. Soon, noise from the raindrops slows to a sharp pitter-patter and then stops. The cloudburst is over.

With the rain silent, but the sky still groaning and echoing around the distant mesas, I peel the plastic back, stretching as I stand up. Everything's wet and glistening.

The scent of fresh rain and sagebrush hang heavy in the misty air. I breathe it in, slowly. The open desert across the street shines at me with wet happiness.

I shake the rainwater off the plastic, still sniffing the perfume air. I shake it harder, making sure the big drops are gone. Folding it in half, and half again, I carry it back to the garage. Tiptoeing to Daddy's workbench—next to the door into the kitchen, where Grace and Mama's voices murmur on the other side—I sit it down quietly, next to Daddy's jars of nails and cans of paint. I back slowly out of the garage. Just like a lizard, no one can tell I had been there.

Happy from my adventure, I run back around the house and through the front door to tell Mama what I'd done. But she and Grace are *still talking*; and hadn't noticed that I'd left.

"Mama!" I yell, jumping up and down. "Guess! Guess what I did!" Her eyes catch mine, but she waves me away.

"Not now, I'm talking to Grace."

The air was heavy, blue with smoke. A line of it spiraled upward from her hand toward the ceiling. I stood there, red-faced, waiting, waiting to tell her—the miracle of that dry spot—right in the driveway. But neither of them glance at me again.

Even without the plastic, Mama doesn't notice me. With my big adventure still on my lips, I wander off again to find someone else to tell it to, or something else to do.

CHAPTER 9

Terry & Sue

Terry Baker ran over me on his bike, Mama. Right smack over me. Remember that day? You weren't there. I didn't like him. He was a mean boy. His bike left a dusty tire track on my dark navy blue jumper. I saw it when I took it off later. The dusty mark started down by my knee and went up across my body to my shoulder. You could look at it, follow the mark it made across my jumper, and see the whole story of what happened.

I was in kindergarten. At the end of the school day, the bell would ring. I'd come out of the building, down the long steep school sidewalk, and follow the crosswalk across the street. Then I'd turn left and keep walking until I found a sign that read "Birch Street;" B-I-R-C-H Street. Here, I'd follow the sidewalk to our house.

But this day with Terry was different. The bell rang, so I walked out of the classroom, and down the steep sidewalk. I'm walking through other kids and parents looking for kids, when suddenly a bike is whizzing *up* the sidewalk, toward me, and on top of it is a boy with dark hair and big, black-framed glasses. Terry Baker. He's a second grader, shorter than me, and a big troublemaker. And somehow he's riding fast, his face a blur, peddling hard, before he flattens me. I'm wearing my favorite navy blue jumper with the gold buttons down the front, and a white lace blouse underneath it. My jumper and I go under the bike, and then there I am, screaming, flat on the sidewalk, blood gushing out of my nose all over my jumper. A sharp ache fills my head where it smacked the sidewalk. Someone comes. A lady. She puts out her hand and I take it, as she wraps an arm around me and slowly helps me stand up.

"Honey, are you okay?" Crying and shaking, I nod bravely, trying to stand as she glances at the boy.

"I'm Sue. I've seen you here at school." I nod again. Then, Sue turns away, yelling, her face red and angry.

"What are you doing riding your bike on the sidewalk?"

"You know that's not allowed on school property!"

"Where's your mom? I'm going to talk to her."

"Look what you just did to her! You tell her you're sorry!"

I turn and look at her, shocked, not from being run over, but from her. She's yelling at Terry Baker! Mouth hanging open, I stop crying and watch her.

Did he say sorry? I don't think so. Terry Baker wasn't a kid who'd be sorry for anything. But that was okay, though, because Sue suddenly is.

That's her name; Sue Kitchen. She lets go of my hand, and pulls out a handkerchief from her purse, and gently swabs my nose with it. Brushing off my jumper, and with one last glare at Terry Baker, Sue holds my hand and leads me to her car and sits me next to her son Jason, and drives me home. She lives on our street too, she says. I bet she doesn't take long naps every day.

I point to our house, and she slows down and pulls into our driveway, and we get out of the car while Jason waits in the backseat. You must have been up already, Mama, and heard a car pull into the driveway because you came to the front door, touching a hand to your hair as we walked up.

"Hi, I'm Sue," Sue says. "Your daughter just got hurt by a boy as she left school. She was walking down the sidewalk to the crosswalk, and he ran right over her on his bike." Sue walks toward the door as if to come in, but you open it just slightly and nod, so I slip through and turn around. Sue stands there, surprised, not sure what to do.

"Oh," you say. "Okay, thank you. I hope she wasn't too much trouble. She can be."

"Trouble?" says Sue, looking carefully at Mama. "Oh no, she wasn't the troublemaker. I was glad I saw what happened and could help." Sue stands there for a moment and hesitates as Mama stiffly holds the screen door. Sue glances down at me through the screen as I watch her. I smile back a little.

"I hope your head is okay. That was quite a knock you took." She looks up steadily at Mama for a few moments. "You might have someone look at that bump. It caused quite a nosebleed."

She says this to you, Mama, and you nod your head slightly but say nothing more. Sue turns around to go, and I try to wave to her, but you close the front door instead.

"Come on," you say, and silently walk down the hallway, toward the bathroom. I take a breath and follow your pursed lips, your towering figure.

"Take your jumper off, and put your pajamas on. Leave your jumper here on the floor, and then go to your room and rest. I need to start fixing dinner."

Taking my jumper off, I see the tire tracks once more riding across the front. I leave it on the bathroom floor. Pulling my pajamas on, I walk silently down the hall, to my room. Sandi isn't home yet. It's just me and Mama.

Torn now—I wanted Mama to be mad like Sue—I climb up on my bed. I think about Sue. I want to walk down to her house, even in my pajamas, and sit next to her on her couch. Instead, I pick up my Casper and hug him close, curling up with him on my pillow. I think of the lady who helped me. Today, Sue, you are my hero— you protected me as I hid behind you, shaken but safe, while you shouted at Terry Baker. You stuck up for me and yelled at a mean boy.

And other girls saw you too, saw a boy hurt a girl, saw a mother not let him get away with it.

CHAPTER 10

Splinters Of The Body

I'm lying across my mother's lap, my bottom bared to her hands.

Later on, there is the older mother.

Now, though, I'm six years old, and scared. My jeans are pulled down, and I'm sobbing, gasping for breath.

"Hold still!" hisses Mama through clenched teeth, rolling the sleeves of her blue denim shirt up, freeing her arms. I try to look at her, but can't see her face over my shoulder.

A bolt of pain screams down my leg. "Aahh!" I yell, as Mama pulls long, wooden splinters out of the soft flesh somewhere near my bottom.

Just a few minutes earlier, I was outside sliding down a piece of scratchy plywood that the neighborhood kids and I found in the alley behind our backyard. We carried it through the gate and leaned it up against a fence. Suddenly, we had a slide. No one saw us put Daddy's ladder next to it, climb up it to the fence top, and slide down it. No one was around.

I stop kicking and wiggling, and lay still across Mama's lap, aching with pain.

"There's more. Hold still!" Mama pulls a two-inch plywood shard out.

"Aaahhh!" I scream again, and flop down, exhausted.

Twisting my head around, I see down to my legs, where a stream of blood runs brightly down them, pooling on the floor.

~

A few weeks ago, our old dog Blackie had gone missing, and after days of looking for him, shouting his name up and down streets, Daddy said, "Well, he must have gone somewhere to die." That's all he said one night at dinner, but I took a quick breath and looked up at him. I waited for him to say more. He didn't. Mama looked up from her plate and frowned silently at Daddy. But she didn't say anything, either.

It was true Blackie was gone, and he hadn't come back. Blackie loved to play. He was black, with a soft, furry brown belly and white paws, and when he wagged his shaggy tail, his whole body wagged, too. And he disappeared, just like that, like he'd never even been our dog for years.

I missed him. I looked for Blackie for a long time. When we got in the car to go anywhere, I rolled my window down and stuck my head out in the wind, looking back behind us, back down the street. He wasn't anywhere.

The night Daddy said Blackie wandered off to

die, I was alone in my room sitting with Casper. And I thought: Mama and Daddy are really old. Suddenly, I get what it means—my whole family is older than me, and they'll die before I do. I'll be the last one. I'll be alone.

Such a bad thought! It's too bad to tell to anyone. Will Sandi still be alive when I die? Will I know I'm dying when it's happening? Will it hurt?

~

These thoughts come flooding back to me while I'm almost upside down, still staring at the floor from Mama's lap, my legs throbbing. I want to get down and run away, but I don't know where I'd go.

Mama says to hold still, but I might be dying right now. Is this what it feels like?

I'll never know why, Mama, but my words just spill right out:

"Mama, are you going to die?"

Your hands stop moving; your elbows stop mid-air. My world holds its breath.

"Why, should I?" you say angrily. "Do you want me to?"

A chill blows across me as I hang limply. My world shakes wildly. And then, somehow, the splinters are out and cleaned up, and she slides me down off her lap. Still wobbling and dizzy, I look up at her face, at her short black hair that she's running a hand through now. She's rolling her shirt sleeves back down, turning to go. She glances down, and sighing, walks toward the kitchen. My legs rubbery, I watch her go.

What just happened, Mama? Are you mad because of the slide? Because I asked about dying? If it's the dying part, it's mostly Daddy's fault. He told us at dinner.

Do you think I want you to die? I feel sick, thinking maybe you do. I want to tell you something, but you're gone and my voice has flown away, stolen by that cold wind on your breath, Mama. That wind took my voice to a trickster; the mean coyote that Navajo kids here say goes around making trouble for everyone. He takes things and breaks things, and makes people fight, then he runs off laughing.

~

At times in my life, I'd drive or fly hundreds of miles to see you in your house by the creek that you and my father built before he died suddenly. Each time, I was sure that things with you would be different. I'd have a plan. We'd sit outside on the patio in the falling evening light and talk, over a piece of cake you'd made. At the right moment, I'd mention some problem I had as a child, or a hard time I'd been through recently. You'd listen, maybe startled, but you'd listen. You'd respond in some way. It'd be a start. We'd feel a bit closer. I'd feel relieved. The plan seemed simple.

But when I'd visit, something darkly magical happened the moment I stepped over the threshold into your house: your old coyote trickster would pop in, from some shadowy cottonwood tree by the creek. He'd take my voice and courage again, and run with them into the dense, wild brush. He'd return them, dancing gleefully the moment I crossed back over that threshold to drive home, laughing crazily as he ran into the dusky evening along the creek's edge.

Right after you said:

"I wish you could have stayed longer. I wish we had a chance to talk more." To my own surprise, I'd find myself saying, "Me too, Mama. Maybe we can next time."

Who you are and how you were with me has been a koan, a Buddhist soul-searching riddle I've turned over in my mind like a stone, grasping at meanings by closing my eyes and feeling with my fingers and my heart around the shapes of all the edges. Working this stone over the years, I tested its prickly and cool shape against different ideas and reasons. Those years were about trying to understand the archetypal story of you and me, mother and youngest daughter, about deciphering that old mythic code, as if by doing that, a door would swing open. A door into a better place, an honesty I kept trying to get to with you.

Your trickster won. I never did ask why you spoke to an injured child that way, or if you remembered it. But what happened with the plywood slide mattered, because that incident stood for so many others with you—shocking, abrupt, silently dismissed. The tall, dark-haired silent woman you were in a frayed, blue bathrobe, through a child's eyes, held such tension, and moved with frightening force.

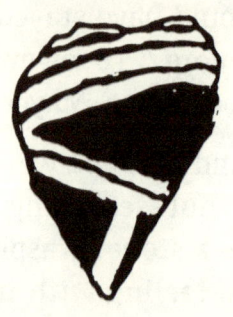

CHAPTER 11

Splinters Of The Heart

You're the older mother now.

I'm your youngest daughter, now sixty years old.

We're so much older, Mama, our skin toughened by the sun, our bodies shaped by our lives. I'm here at your assisted living home, just from the airport. Sandi is here with me, too.

We hurry inside; then, mindful of where we are, we slow down and look for someone to talk to. A nurse hears the door close, and steps out of the kitchen, walking over. Recognizing us, she nods solemnly. "Just go on in. We've been watching over her. You know she's not able to speak or move. Your sister Donna is with her."

We leave the nurse, hesitating, and turn toward your room, as Donna appears in the hallway, her face shuttered, shaking her head slowly. The three of us walk to your doorway.

I'm here, Mama.

I pause at the doorway, feeling into the silence of your room. My eyes slowly adjust to the dim lighting. I see your outline under a blanket on your bed. You lay quietly, eyes closed, your body slowly closing down; lingering, maybe, for this moment, for me and Sandi to arrive.

The still air in the room holds a somber but peaceful energy that pulls me in. Wanting to be closer to you, I slide a chair from the desk next to you, where your head rests on the pillow, and sit down. My hand reaches out of its own accord to touch your wrist lightly. It is cool to the touch.

I'm here, Mama.

You don't respond to my touch, or move in any way that I see. Yet my quiet heart and body resonate with your heart and body, and I am all love and tenderness for you, Mama; it surrounds us, it breathes us both, it fills this room. How fragile your thin body is, how still you are, how hard you struggle to breathe. How slowly your breath comes now.

How glad I am to be here.

I'm so glad I made it here in time.

My heart breaks watching you take long, ragged breaths, and breaks again as you exhale each one, but

I don't look away. Your breaths—I count them—keep coming and I am still here with you, and for the first time across an arc of sixty years, you don't send me away—you're beyond words—and I am simply with you, with each breath, and there is nothing else to do at all but this.

Only this. Being here with you.

I want time to slow even more, as I drink in how I'm touching you, and you don't pull away. I want to stay like this.

And now I want time to stop.

Years of conversations I longed for with you, stories left unspoken inside me, rise up in my throat all at once—whole periods of my life—rise like a cresting tide, then flow outward, knowing I see and feel them all, just by being here with you, resting my hand on your arm. Something lets go inside of me. It's enough.

Mama, you've offered a last chance, but I don't know if you meant to. You've held on for days, with little food or water. And so here we are, your daughters gathered up next to you. You, who shunned attention, are surrounded by it, as we sit together around your bed, holding watch. You've waited and now we're here with you, in this last great mystery, maybe unfolding it in your own way.

Is this, your final act of silence, a gift? Did you feel my blessings encircle you from the Santuario?

I'll never know, Mama.

It doesn't matter, because Donna and Sandi and I are all here.

I touch your arm again, sending you love. We're here together, in this luminous warmth for these precious, final hours. I sense your body taking in this loving—just for this moment, as Donna sits at your feet, and Sandi sits across from me.

I pull out one of my favorite old book club books from my bag, *The Wizard of Oz*. Opening it up to the middle, I read a few pages from where Dorothy and her three friends have arrived at the Emerald City, but then I decide to stop.

I take my WI-FI speaker out instead and cue up Ella Fitzgerald singing *They Can't Take That Away From Me*. She quietly sings as the orchestra flitters angelically around her voice. I look up at Sandi, who forces a wan smile from across the bed, as we listen to music we've heard all our lives. Sandi's long look catches me, and I pause the music, setting the speaker aside.

I'm already missing everything that happened between us, and everything that never did. I'm missing the whole mess of it. My one-sided relationship with you—talked about with sisters, but not with you. I wanted to know all the stories of you—what made you happy, and what made you so sad, so dark.

I wanted the certainty of your love, one that caught and held me, that was steady when I wasn't. But being here is worth this terrible realness, because there is steadiness here. A steadiness so vast it holds all our family's messiness and struggles.

I never answered you that awful day long ago, Mama, when you asked if I wanted you to die. But heeding the wisdom of the hospice nurse, I bend down to your ear.

"Mama. Go when you need to. We know it's time. It's okay."

I am grateful, Mama, that you waited for me to come and be here with you. But you are free to go.

CHAPTER 12

The Dark Night After

I stayed at your house with Sandi. We got back that night, to find the Virgin of Guadalupe candle I'd lit for you sputtering on the fireplace hearth, even though there was plenty of wax left. When we finally went to bed, it was out. The house seemed darker, emptier, without it. Wherever you were now, you weren't there. Maybe that was you, though, later that night, when Sandi smelled smoke and got up to check. She walked around outside the house in the dark, hearing coyotes howling, but the smoky smell was only inside. But there was nothing lit, nothing there.

~

Those first days after, I thought about the mother

we'd cared for, my heart glad and broken, too ragged to make sense of anything.

Mama was almost forty when I was born, I mused. My friends' parents were a decade younger. That had always seemed strange. Maybe too many years passed, with two daughters a dozen years older than me and Sandi. It was almost a new family. I wondered if having us was even a choice.

By my late twenties, counseling and self-help books had taught me more about behavior, and the importance of early childhood. There wasn't a single answer to who Mama was, each person is a labyrinth, and hers ran deeply into places where we were not invited to follow. She was an odd combination, both sad and sharp. Maybe an upside-down sort of narcissist, someone who felt terribly oppressed, but never spoke it, or sought out help of any kind, as far as I knew.

By forty, those years of Indian philosophy and Tibetan Buddhist practices had softened me, and I was looking for a way out of the legal profession. And the teachings also sent me travelling to the places where they had first arisen, to understand how people there lived them from the inside out. The simple humility of people shown in their faces and gestures, throughout Tibet and Nepal; it seemed to emanate from the spiritual leaders in the temples, through the villages and into families there. Families were cohesive, and cared for one another in a way I had never experienced. Questions about Mama vanished, as I took in these simple examples of love for self and other that the teachings transmitted. Mama seemed then like a cosmic blip, that through a divine biological exchange, she had birthed me into a life to unfold the map of my soul. If I had chosen her as my mother, I could trust that life would reveal more in time. The teachings flourished in this fertile soil, and a deeper peace born out of my own insights emerged.

And yet, the old mother-ache returned.

And there was that ancient memory. I had been forwarned that this life would be hard, that I must find a way to fully live it. My mother and I were two humans miles apart when we stood next to each another. I kept visiting, and trying to talk. The years kept passing.

And now, she was gone.

CHAPTER 13

Plans

"It'd be an honor to officiate at your mother's memorial service," says the pastor of Mama's church. The cell phone connection muffles in and out. "I'm sorry for your loss. I knew of your mother, that she needed full-time care and couldn't come to worship services the last few years, so I never met her. I'm sure you miss her terribly, but I hope you take comfort knowing she is embraced in the arms of the Lord her Savior."

I'm silent on the other end of the phone, uncertain what to say to this man I haven't met, who seems to have a speech ready. My sisters had suggested I call him. I wondered if the thought of Mama embraced by the Lord had ever occurred to them. I was pretty sure it hadn't.

"Hello? Are you still there?"

"Yes, I'm here," I say. "Maybe I should tell you more about her, about her life. About our family."

"Yes, I'd like to hear."

"Well, if you were to ask me or my two sisters

about her, the first thing we'd all say would be some version of: 'She wasn't the easiest mother by a long shot.' All her life, she was quite a private woman who didn't talk much on her best days. Her mental state had deteriorated the last few years, so I feel a bit relieved for her, frankly, that her struggles are over. She was very unhappy living away from her house, so it was hard all the way around. I'm not sure we miss her yet. I guess right now we're all more numb and exhausted than sad. It took a toll. But she's been on our minds so long we don't know what to do with ourselves, either, with no one to look after. It's left a hole."

"I understand that. You've gotten so used to thinking of her, of watching over her. But I'm also very glad for her that she had three daughters to look after her. She was blessed that way."

"Yes. She was surely fortunate. We weren't close growing up, especially the oldest two with the youngest two. There were four of us kids. Our oldest sister died quite a while ago. The only thing Mama ever said about a service was that she wanted to be cremated. We're planning a memorial service at the funeral home and will bury her with my father. We'll have a party at her house afterward. We're keeping the house until the spring party, on what would have been her ninety-fifth birthday."

"What a nice tribute for your whole family!"

"Well, so many of our kids came and stayed there, and, before that, we sisters visited. I'm guessing a few other family or friends may come, and we thought it'd be a bit of a reunion there. She loved family gatherings and would love it that people came to her house for a final send-off. We'll set out photos of her life. She was in the Navy during World War II and had a special clearance to carry mail between the White House and the Pentagon. We'll set pictures out from those years, too. We were proud of her for that. And my sisters would like a twenty-one gun salute at the cemetery, given Mama was a veteran. She would definitely love that one."

"It sounds like she had a pretty full life."

"You know, I suppose she did, although we only heard snippets about it. We've pieced some of it together, but not that much, considering she was our mother, and there were four of us. And, also... I'd hope we sisters are able at the service to express not just memories that we treasure, but the harder memories with her, too. It was we three that got each other across that finish line these last years, not a loving connection with Mama, to be honest. Although still, I surely did love her. Does that shock you to hear?"

The silence at the other end of the phone grew heavy as I waited for him to respond.

"No. No, actually, it doesn't. In my own life, I had to overcome a lot of personal pain with my father. He was an alcoholic, and it tore our family apart. I went into military service as a way to escape my home life, but I found a calling to the Lord there and went to seminary afterward. I've always credited my father with that, or, I suppose, my healing of that relationship created the desire to help others and to serve the Lord in our small towns here. So your idea of a service that expresses caring, but honest thoughts about a parent is important to include, and I believe makes for a better service. We'll give time for each of you to say whatever you want to."

"I'll talk to my sisters about it. There are other things about Mama that my sisters will want to share, but the service isn't until spring, so we'll talk again."

"Yes, let's talk more after you visit with your family about whatever's important to them."

"One final thing. While my sisters might say they were Christian—I'm not sure—I'm more of a Buddhist. There may well be family members and others there from different backgrounds, so I'm hoping to have a service where everyone feels welcomed."

"Well, I'll do my best to prepare a service that fits all of you. In your beliefs, and in the latitude of saying whatever is best, for each of you to share if you choose."

"Thank you, Pastor. This has been helpful to sort out with you. We'll be back in touch soon."

I reach both of my sisters by phone that evening.

"Well, I don't know about that talking part. I just want it over with," says Donna, now the oldest. Long ago I had thought of her as kind, but much had happened since then.

Including the death of Lynn, Mama's first, and favorite. Christmas was spent at Lynn's house, and Mama would stay a month or more. Lynn's sudden death one evening was a shock. The news came when I was shopping for groceries.

"Lynn's dead," my no-longer-kind sister Donna says when I pull my cart aside to answer my cell phone.

"She was watching a movie, probably drinking, and fell over on the couch and died. Her husband found her later and called the ambulance, but it was too late. I just can't believe it! Well, now you know. Mama asked me to call. She's a mess. She was going there in a couple of weeks for Christmas and was already packed. Call her soon. I have to go."

Dazed, I exhale and look around me. I wheel my cart to the nearest checkout to pay for my groceries. Fumbling in my purse for my wallet, I say something to the cashier as I hand her my credit card. "Thank you! Do you want your receipt?" she asks. I look at her, lost in thought, and forget what to do next. "Here's your bag," she says, looking closely at me.

"Oh, right, thanks," I mumble as I take it, walk out of the store, and burst into tears.

She what?—I ask myself, as I walk to my car. *She died? How could she just die, just like that?* I'd made an uneasy truce with myself a couple of years prior about her drinking and didn't call her after that, but she hadn't seemed to notice.

Then a thought comes: *maybe now there's a chance for the rest of us. Maybe we three can sort out those old arguments she started and liked to keep going.*

That night, I turn my bed down, thinking of Lynn and our mixed, sad relationship. I slip into the comfort of the soft, warm sheets. Resting quietly, my breathing slows as I drift off. At the twilight edge of sleep, a vision arises. Meditation had, in time, relaxed the filters through which I saw all of life. At times these visions naturally arose, unbidden but clear. They came most often in my waking hours, but sometimes they came at the edge of sleep. I'd ignored them, but eventually, yogic and Tibetan teachers taught me to relax, to absorb and hold them. They were great gifts—teachings, they said, in a type of cosmic language.

I'm lying in bed at the edge of sleep. Thoughts of Lynn, scenes from her life dance before me, but now bathed in love. I then seem to be falling upward. My body dissolves into bright nothing as I rise. Now columns of flowing light are surrounding me; columns that seem to be made up of stars. I am floating gently upward through this tunnel of starry light. A light of pure love and warmth infuses me. I move as only awareness with no body through the tunnel. Far ahead, I see beyond the tunnel, to an open, star-filled cosmos. Suddenly, I seem to leap toward the open cosmos, and in the same moment, awaken. Lying in bed, I feel the dreamy, full sense of love surround me, and fall asleep, grateful for these moments beyond my surface understanding.

~

"I don't know that I'll have much to say about her at the service." Donna's tone is sharp on the phone. "But you two can say whatever you want. I have to live here, around people in the town who knew us both. You don't. It was bad enough being around her. I don't know if I want to drag up all that I went through in front of everybody."

"Well, sure," I say. "You don't have to say anything, but you can if you change your mind. You were around her the most in the last years, so thought you might want to."

"Well, I'll say a few words," Sandi says. "I like the idea. Mentioning the harder things, but with the good parts, too. Not pretending she was better, or worse than she was, because we all did too much of that, just like she did."

Sandi calls me back, after the three of us sign off.

"I'm so glad we cleared things up between us. We missed out on so much of each other's lives. You missed getting to know my kids. I missed knowing your daughter. Mom was so shut down, I was angry with her, and didn't want to come see her, so I missed seeing you too for years. My not-a-twin sister."

"Oh, Sandi, me too." Her words caught me by surprise. "Those were some hard talks we had. But we hung in there and had them. I can't believe we rehashed things back to when we were little. But we didn't learn about making up and getting along from Mama, so I guess we had to teach that to ourselves. But I understand more, from your point of view."

"Yeah, it's been nice. And it made it fun at times, to help Mama out these last years. Even Donna came to count on our help. I'll miss the times we three talked about her care, or looked after her house, and could still have a laugh once in a while about it all. It wasn't easy, but we had a common mission, and we got to spend time together in a new way, too."

"Yeah, I feel that way, too, Sandi. I'm so glad it's changed. And it'll be fun again, planning the party after the service with you."

The silence on the phone this time was sweet and long. I could hear her breathing, and I knew she felt exactly the same way that I did.

"You know, we haven't talked about this, but when we were little, did you ever wonder why Mama almost never got out of the car when we went for a drive?"

"Oh, yeah, Sandi, I have. I wondered about it for years."

CHAPTER 14

Your Silent Feet

Mama, why do your feet look like that? I want to know, but I'm scared to ask. Can I ask you? No. You'll get mad. I look at your toes, and they look wrong to my five-year-old eyes. They're pink and squished. They're curled up and hiding, back against your foot. Seeing them makes my stomach jump. My toes are pink, and not squished together like that. Do they hurt?

Standing next to you in your bathroom, a place I hardly ever get to see, feels like a good secret. I watch as you sit down on the toilet lid to put your sock on. Then you put a dark blue canvas shoe over it. You wince as you slide it on.

"Mama, can I tie your shoe? Can I?" I want to, and you say yes and let me. I tie shoes fast now and want to show you, but thinking of your squished toes inside your shoe makes my hands shake a little. Left over right, and pull it tight. There. You sigh and stand up but don't look at me. You walk into your bedroom. I follow. I always follow you, Mama.

I'm twelve, and I'm setting the dinner table one evening, putting the plates and glasses down, when you suddenly mention shoes that were too small.

"I didn't have new shoes to start each school year. I usually had to wear my old ones that were too small. Put this platter over there for me, and then you're done."

You say it like I'd tell you I was going for a bike ride. That's all you say—your shoes were too small and you had to wear them anyway. I glance at your face and decide not to ask more. You look sad, Mama, and whatever hangs in the air around you is there a lot, a wall that makes it hard to ask anything.

But questions about your feet and shoes won't be quiet in my head. I want to ask them.

Why didn't someone buy you bigger shoes?

Mama, did you tell your mama that your shoes hurt your feet?

~

I'm at an election law conference years later near your Indiana hometown, so I decide to take an extra day, and I stop in to visit my uncle—your brother. You were excited for me to see him, since I hadn't seen Uncle Dave for close to twenty years. Maybe because I'm here without you—I'm on a business trip, so you didn't come—a surprising puzzle piece turns up. We talk for a while in Uncle Dave's kitchen over a late lunch before the subject turns to your mother, my Grandma J.

Suddenly he says: "You know, once Mother left your mom and I, and she was gone so long that by the time she came back, I didn't know who she was."

"What?" I say. "Really? You're kidding me. I've never heard that before."

"Yes, she did. She left both of us with different relatives. The only reason I saw my big sister after that—your mother—was because she came by my house each morning and walked me to school. She did that for years. Then one day at home when I was a young boy I heard a knock at the door, and I went to open it. A lady stood there, smiling at me. I looked at her, waiting to hear what she wanted. 'Dave,' she said, 'don't you know your own mother?' Then she laughed. Like it was my fault I didn't know her."

"What a shock that must have been! I had no idea. I'm sorry, Uncle Dave."

Smiling sadly, your brother looked at me, nodded slowly, then shook his head in disbelief. He sat in his chair, his face a shadow of that younger boy again. Then he picked up his beer, emptied the glass, and slammed it down on the kitchen table.

~

This silence is how it was, Mama; silent decades—sheer cliffs of blackness, where the light of what I knew about you dropped off into nothing, too far down to see the bottom. You'd toss out a sentence or two at odd times about your early life, then retreat from saying more, as you leaped across that twilight abyss of words back into darkness. As if a ghost might be after you, might punish you for speaking out loud about your life, but couldn't catch you if you were still and silent. Sometimes when my sisters and I visited you, you'd talk a little about yourself, and when you did, other conversations stopped mid-word as all heads turned to listen to you, like some exotic birdsong filling ears with snippets of sound about your parents, about things that happened, or that you knew.

Once during a birthday visit like this, you suddenly said, "My mother left me with my dad's parents, and she put my brother with other family. She went to Denver with some man. We didn't see her for four years." We four daughters were sitting at your patio table with you, eating lunch. I'd told my sisters years before what Uncle Dave said about this, so we already knew about her leaving for years. But this part—about going to Denver with a man—was new. A look around the table between us four sisters created an instant, silent agreement to act as if this was all new, hoping you'd say even more. We asked, "What? Why did she go with him? Who was he? Why didn't you all go?"

"Oh, I don't know. I don't really remember. It was so long ago. I have to go turn the sprinkler off out back before it floods the roses," you said and got up and fled the table of wide-eyed silent daughters staring after you, and at each other.

A story piece here and there wrote a new, spotty chapter of your life that in time got rearranged when a new piece dropped in. I became a puzzle-keeper, a riddle-solver. But I wasn't good at guessing answers with so many missing pieces.

~

I'm in my early forties. It's your eightieth birthday and my sisters and I are gathered once again at your house to celebrate this milestone with you. It's evening, and we're having snacks with some wine, and Lynn had poured you a rare, second glass. We're outside at the patio table when you tell us that because you were "a tall gal"—exactly six feet tall—in the nineteen-thirties, it was hard to find shoes in your size. Women were shorter and had smaller feet, you supposed. Your mother worked at Toby's, the neighborhood tavern, and was out late most nights, too; you spent your grade school years wandering between the houses of grandparents and aunts.

"But Mama, when did your parents divorce? How old were you?"

"I have no idea. No one told me. I was small. No one talked about that."

A silent, well-behaved child, a dark-haired pretty girl who curled up on a couch and spent the night wherever she fell asleep; your night-going mother never missing you.

You never complained, never said a word, and the aunts and grandparents didn't notice that, over and over, you'd outgrown your shoes. You kept wearing them.

"But Mama, in some pictures you have such nice clothes on, " I say. "Didn't you have shoes to match them?"

"My grandmother and aunts took in laundry and did ironing for the wealthier families in town. The families gave my aunts hand-me-downs, and they cut them down for me. We all could sew."

You tell us that when your parents divorced, your father never paid child support, or helped your mother in any way. You only visited him at his out-of-state house a handful of times.

You didn't know him.

We didn't either.

The second glass of wine at your birthday dinner loosened you and gave us these stories. The next morning, your face has that darkly closed look again.

"There's a pot of coffee. I'm going out back to water," you say, breezing past me. You say nothing about what you'd shared the night before, and I never again saw you have a second glass of wine.

But one piece of your life now made a bit more sense.

~

I think of your feet now like the feet of Chinese women, who, for millennia, had them bound up as young girls to keep them small. Their families believed this painful, disfiguring practice made women more beautiful; that it would bring blessings in the form of a good marriage. Generations of women's feet suffered this way—prisoners of a strange ideal, one that equated beauty with smallness. One that kept women still and quiet inside houses—kept them from fluidly moving through their lives.

Your feet were not imprisoned for a cultural idea of beauty, but disfigured by poverty, and your absent mother, who didn't notice that your shoes had been oh-so-tight for way too long. When you were old enough to buy larger shoes on your own, your toes had already retreated, deciding for themselves to keep your feet small.

Your feet held their own kind of silence for so many years, Mama.

How can I redeem them for you? At sixty, and also six feet tall, my own feet have many pains that live in them. Pains not caused by small shoes, but that have slowed me down all the same, Mama, taken away my far wanderings into high, alpine wildflower-scented places; into remote, sandstone canyons where ancient voices whisper softly when the earth's stillness is just right.

Feet that slow me, but never stop me.

I keep hiking, though. I glance over now and then, seeing you in the clouds, in the high desert rains that fall but never touch the ground, moving easily on a breath of wind, an exhale from spirit goddesses. As my own feet heal, I don't wince—as you once did—when I set them down on the floor. And as they heal, from wherever you are, you smile at me, across the timeless horizon of memory.

CHAPTER 15

A Homecoming

"I hear cars pulling up. At least we had a head start from the cemetery. I'll move the appetizers outside. The chairs are already up." Sandi glanced around at kitchen counters filled with plates of bite-size sandwiches brimming with cheese and meat. "I'm glad the cafe could whip up a sandwich platter so quickly."

Donna nodded as she arranged carrots on a platter next to the hummus and celery. She paused and looked up. "The service went well," she said. "The cemetery burial, too. Not many people, but she'd outlived almost everyone."

"I wish Aunt Margie had been able to come. Not many people left in Mama and Daddy's old hometown in Indiana, either, except Aunt Margie." Sandi's eyes found mine, and I nodded as she went on. "At least from their generation, there isn't. She's been in my thoughts. I'd love to see her. She has all the old family history and good stories about Daddy growing up. I guess she's not able to travel these days."

"I loved our summer visits back there when we were little." I pause against the kitchen door, warmed by the memories.

" Yeah, I did too. I didn't expect anyone from there or from the Glen Canyon area to make it, but Ron did." Sandi looked thoughtful. "Ron was about the only one of Mama and Daddy's friends left from those early dam-building days."

"But people important to her these last years from around town were there."

"I jumped when those guns went off. I thought of Mama, marching in a platoon. What a picture! And women her age, in World War II. But she was a part of that." I look up at my sisters, but the silence is heavy. Donna finished peeling the carrots and glanced up from the platter. "Yeah. I guess women got out of the house because of the war. That probably helped Mama."

"She got forced out of her shell a little, I added."

"I wonder what people thought of what I said, though." Donna looked up anxiously. "I guess I'll hear about it around town. I said some not charming things, but they'll get it. I don't care. She just wanted so much out of everyone. What a mix she was. She could be so hard, but she sure loved those silly old Hollywood movies—at least until a couple of years ago."

"That's true. We watched *The Wizard of Oz* every year. She liked it more than we did. And Cary Grant, Clark Gable, all the old actors. We'd watch a lot of movies when I came over. We weren't really talking, but still. Once she told me she went alone all the time to matinees as a kid because tickets were so cheap. I got the feeling it helped her get by."

"It went well, but I'm glad it's over." Sandi stepped into the kitchen carrying a cutting board, washing it off in the kitchen sink. "I cried before I went up to the podium, but I gave Mama an honest send-off. I think she'd get it."

"Yeah. It was hard to find the line between saying how it was, and what was good about it," I added. "But once I said the hard stuff, better things came to mind. Like how we were always outside as kids, so I fell in love with the desert. With plants. And lizards. I remembered how she'd save hiking articles for me. I felt good about it by the end. I didn't want to pretend."

"She did that smiley, 'good Mama' face to the world so much. I guess it worked if you didn't live with her." Donna grimaced as she went outside.

"Boy, that's true," I said. "A couple of my kid friends really liked her. But she sure didn't like everyone. I had a teacher—my first one, Mrs. Smith—that I loved, and I still remember how Mama was really cold to her the whole year. Even as a kid, I felt like I had to hide how much I liked Mrs. Smith! Hadn't thought of that in forever."

Silence hangs over the kitchen, except for the sounds of knives chopping vegetables. Sandi catches my eye again. "The photo movie we put together was amazing! Those pictures of her before we were all born. She was so gorgeous. I cried again when Louis Armstrong sang *What A Wonderful World*. I don't know why she liked that song. She was so unhappy."

"Maybe she felt that way back then," I said.

"Maybe." Sandi shrugged.

I took a breath. "So, Donna, your kids decided not to come."

Donna looked up from the doorway, then turned sharply, dropping her cutting board into the sink with a loud clatter. "They came when she had pneumonia last time to help me out. They didn't need to be here."

"Well, that was a year ago." I could feel Sandi's eyes on us both. "And, we're here, too. And our families, for the service and party. And Grant came."

Donna stood perfectly still, shadowed against the kitchen sink. "They didn't *want* to come. I didn't think they needed to, either." She shut off the faucet, picked up a kitchen towel, and dried her hands as she walked briskly out back, staring straight ahead.

"Guess the truce is over." Sandi looked sideways at me, and nodded.

"Never was one. Just a pause to help Mama. That was all. We never sorted anything out."

~

We jumped at the sound of car doors slamming. I'm carrying the last platter out back, where smiling people are gathering, while others walk up our mother's driveway. It's a strange picture—a party scene unfolding in a house full of dusty furniture; a house where no one has lived for almost three years.

"I wasn't sure we could keep the house long enough to have the memorial party here today." I walked over to where Sandi was quickly folding napkins. "Hard to believe it'd be her ninety-fifth birthday. I guess we had the idea because we've come out for her birthday each year for ages. Mama never wanted to do much, but I'll miss the hiking and hanging out. I love it here. We'll sell it soon enough." Sandi nods sadly.

A few familiar faces, and many that aren't, walk through the carport breezeway into the backyard, talking together. A tall woman with short, curly gray hair and an easy smile stops by the appetizer table, and then walks over toward me and Sandi.

"Well, hello, you two. I'm Dot. Glad to meet you, finally. I've heard about you from your mother. I've met Donna a couple of times, but not either of you that I recall. I drive the rural medical transport van. I picked up your mom for years, sometimes once a week, before she went to live at the assisted living place."

"Oh, sure," I said. "I've heard about you, too. She liked riding in your van; I think it was kind of a sightseeing trip. She didn't get out much after her eyesight failed. We were so glad the county funded it."

"Yeah! It was quite the big news when we started. Lots of people ride it. I got your mom to and from a lot of appointments. She was a quiet lady, but she just kept on going. She slowed down, but still got on and off by herself. She was proud of that.

I heard you girls talk at the service. You knew your mom differently than I did, but she was friendly to me, and always on time. But what I really want you to know was what an enduring spirit she had, an independence that never stopped. She lost her husband, and then I watched her lose most of her vision, and her oldest daughter. She just kept going. It's not easy growing old and living alone."

"Well, you're right, Dot, she did endure," I said. "Yeah. She lost a lot. I'm glad you're reminding us. She sure was independent in her way. I saw her more as secretive, though, or too private. I don't know." I looked over where Sandi stood next to Dot's shoulder, but her face was unreadable. She listened intently.

"She called me a couple times when she fell. She didn't want you girls to know."

"When she fell?" My empty cup tipped over on the table as I sat it down.

"Yeah, I came over at least three times, once when she fell in the carport. She had her cell, so she called. I had to call the firemen to lift her, because I sure couldn't get her up. Those strong men got her right up. After they left, she looked right at me with this deadpan face and said, 'Wow! That was quite a handsome guy I just met!' We got a big laugh out of that one." I look from wide-eyed Sandi to Dot, still grinning, and smile weakly, uncertain of this person who knew our mother this way.

"Dot, that's a great story. We didn't really see our mother like that. I'll be thinking on that one! I'm glad you were there, driving the shuttle. It was a huge help."

"Well, I just wanted to say hi, to introduce myself, and pay my respects to your Mama. I've missed her.

Have a good afternoon," she said, waving to Donna, who joined Sandi and me as Dot walked out through the carport breezeway.

"Hey, y'all! Good sandwiches." Lynn's son, Grant, smiled broadly as he strode across the yard to where we stood. "The guns at the cemetery were awesome! I saw a couple of women in the lineup. Grandma woulda liked that, but she'd have liked this party, too."

"Grant! Hey, so glad you came," I said. "Haven't seen you since your mother's funeral. Such a hard time. Well, this is more of a party. Heard you had a little boy! He's three now? I saw him at the cemetery in his cowboy boots."

"Yeah, he's almost four, and I'm hitting forty-four the week after his birthday. It's weird having him here; I was a kid here. Maybe tomorrow I'll take him over to wade in the creek." Grant looked away for a moment. "You know, I heard you at the service. But when I came out in the summer, I loved it. I'd play and swim in the creek all day. Grandma pretty much left me alone to roam wherever I wanted, eat whenever I wanted. We'd watch old movies at night. I still think about those days. Way better than being stuck at home with my mom. And those humid, buggy Texas summers!"

I glanced over at Sandi, who looked back, unblinking. Apparently being raised by Mama was a world apart from knowing her in other ways.

"You know, Grant, I get that. I think being a grandkid, and a boy, made a huge difference. And I'm glad for you that it did. And that you got to know this place, too."

"Well, I need to help get my boy down for a nap, so we'll see you later."

~

"Looks like everyone's cleared out. Grant just left," Sandi said. "Let's go take a breather. I need to eat something."

My sisters and I walk through the house, rummaging through leftover drinks and food. I bring along a sandwich and iced tea, then settle down at the patio table.

"Knock, knock," a voice called, as Aunt Jean stepped in through the carport door. "Hi, girls! Can I come in? Sorry I didn't make it to the service. I haven't been feeling well, so thought I'd rest and then drop by here."

"Hey! Come in! We're just sitting down to eat. Grab something and come out." I motion her over toward where we've placed the leftovers on the countertop.

"Oh, good! I'll be right there. I don't get to see you all that often, and hardly ever in one spot," she said. Leaning her cane next to the door, she looked over the remaining food platters, picked up a drink and a sandwich, and walked carefully onto the patio.

Aunt Jean sat down slowly, with a sigh. "Glad I caught you. It's nice to be in your mom's house one last time. The backyard looks beautiful, with the roses blooming. I could smell the honeysuckle when I was coming up the driveway. Your mother would be happy you're all here." We sit silently, we three sisters with our aunt, lost in thought.

"Yeah, I think she would be, too." I looked at Aunt Jean and hesitated. "You know, she was hard on us, Aunt Jean. I don't know if you knew that. It was more what she didn't do than what she did. I know you two weren't really close. But I honestly never knew what she thought of me, or anyone, for that matter." Birds sang as we silently ate at the old oak patio table.

"Well...yes," Aunt Jean replied. "She was a quiet one. It always seemed to me she was waiting for the world to come to her door. But the world isn't like that. You have to get out there and find it, and meet it. I told her that once, and she didn't speak to me for weeks."

My sisters and I look at each other but remain silent. Aunt Jean had a way of speaking her mind pretty freely at times, and we'd all heard about this from Mama.

"But I know one thing for sure about her. She loved you! She hardly talked about anything else. *You were her world!* Everything she said was about her girls and her grandkids."

I stared at her, sandwich in hand, my stomach suddenly in knots. "I'm not sure that's true. It sure didn't feel that way to me. You know, she hardly had a good word for any of us, for anything. A high school performance. Job promotion. Graduation. You name it. She couldn't get the words out, like it took something from her if she said it. She didn't talk about us *to us.* Maybe she talked about us *to other people.* To you. I know she did. She bragged at times. It was strange. I never figured it out." My sisters glanced up from their food, their heads nodding wearily.

"I'd say that was true. She'd brag about one of us to the other, too. It didn't exactly make us closer. I don't know why she was like that. It sort of set us against each other." Donna's face looked sad as she fell silent again.

"But I appreciate hearing you say this, Aunt Jean," I said. "And I do think she got happier after my dad died, like a little freedom found her in those years."

"Yes, I think so too," my aunt agreed, thoughtfully nodding her head. "I taught school for a long time before I married your uncle and had a family. I moved and traveled a lot, too. Your mom didn't have that opportunity. Many women didn't. You know, don't you, that your father told her she'd never be able to live here without him? She told me that after he died. He said she couldn't manage this place! Guess she proved him wrong for thirty-five years. He was always telling her what she couldn't do."

"I never heard her say that, but he could be like that. Bossy. Impatient," I said.

"Yes, he was." Donna nodded. "But it was more how he treated her than what he said. His attitude. And, he yelled a lot. Not really at her, but he got mad easily. About almost anything."

Sandi nodded. "I'm not sure my dad thought anyone could do anything as well as he could."

"Uh-huh." I smile at my aunt, who smiled ruefully back. Sandi looks down and shakes her head, smiling. Donna is silent, lost in her own memories. "But, still. Mama never said a word against Daddy in spite of living with that. Not even after he died. Not in those years growing up by the dam, either."

Sandi walked over to the leftovers, and picked up an apple. "Man, those were dusty years, though, that windy mesa in the middle of nowhere. What a nutty place to grow up."

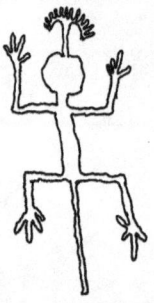

CHAPTER 16

Lizard, My Friend

There is something about the desert... There is something there which the mountains, no matter how grand and beautiful, lack; which the sea, no matter how shining and vast and old, does not have.
~ Edward Abbey

There is a far-away world, towering red rock and cliffs, when I raise my head. But I don't because I'm holding still, looking down, about to catch a lizard. The lizard doesn't know he's going to be caught, but he is. I have a lizard-catching plan, and each time it works, I get better at it. I'm five, and I hardly ever miss now.

The lizard doesn't see me stalking him, step-by-step, and now I use my shadow to scare him toward a clump of Indian Ricegrass. It's soft and won't cut my fingers. He's run into it, turning to squint up at the giant girl following him. I bend down slowly, quietly, waiting like a blue heron fishing a stream. Slowly, slowly. Now on my knees, I shape my left palm and fingers into a fleshy cave.

Bending my forearm down along the red sand next to the clump of tall grass, I form an arm canyon leading to the cave. Holding still, my whole arm becomes a part of the desert floor.

Then I stretch my right hand slowly along the sand to where the lizard is hiding in the grass. I make a small *pshht* sound, enough to make him move. And sure enough, he turns and runs, heading for the safety of my left-hand cave.

Holding my left arm so still, I raise my right hand around me, and slowly bring around a glass jar. I put it in front of my cave hand, which I now wiggle, startling the lizard, who bolts, surprised, right into the jar. It worked!

Jumping up with my glass jar, I dance around. I did it! I did it! Looking next to me, I see the sagebrush. Maybe there's another lizard there. It's hard to catch lizards in sagebrush, though. It's all rough and pokey with thorny branches. I watch my lizard, who watches me back through the glass jar. I tell him he's safe—that I have a nice desert home where I'll put him.

I love my lizards; I love them so much! They are so fast and pretty with all kinds of spots on them. They can run sideways on canyon walls, where they stop to cock their heads and look at me. I love catching them in those wild canyons. I keep them a few days, to watch them. I have a big wooden crate filled with red sand and rocks, with places to hide, and it has a screen on top to keep them in.

I'll put this lizard in there. It's empty today. Later I'll inch along the side of our house, looking for tiny moths that cling to the concrete block walls there. I have a moth-catching plan, too. I lift them gently off, between my thumb and first finger so I don't squish them, and they can still fly. Then I slip them under the screen, into the cage for the lizards to chase and eat. I watch my lizards eat moths and sometimes they smile at me when they look up.

Standing now, I look out toward that far world— the horizon above the sagebrush—and see clear over to the Vermilion Cliffs in the distance. Purple-hued cliffs, with tall shadows that climb up an uneven cliff top. Gazing around from there, I see smaller cliffs in front of those, like deep orange-colored skyscrapers in a big city, only the cliffs are made of red sandstone. Then I see the dark, winding cut in front of them, the cut that drops straight down, so far down, to where huge birds wheel and dive above the Colorado River. Turning more, I see the small, half-moon gray shape of Glen Canyon Dam, holding back the blue lake behind it. And, above the lake, a blue sky from horizon to horizon. A sky so blue there is nothing for it to do except get bluer the higher I look, until suddenly the sky is alive and watching me, as I spin around and see the earth again, over here now, the skyline edges stacked with lighter pink-gray cliffs.

Brushing sand off my shorts and hands, I pick up

my lizard jar. Screwing the top on carefully, I put my eye against the lid and look down at him through breathing holes I punched this morning with an ice pick. Walking along the empty desert to my house, I want to sing! I'm so happy with my lizard! And my desert. The place I love to play. My place.

I'll be home in a minute, and I need to get this lizard into his new crate in the backyard before Mama sees me and makes me turn him loose. Sometimes I sneak the crate into the house, but lizards get out and show up in awful places, like that time on Mama's bed pillow. She really screamed! I love my lizards, but they get me into trouble, too. But I don't care, I love them. They're worth it.

CHAPTER 17

Mrs. Smith and Red, Red Lipstick

You didn't like Mrs. Smith, Mama. You never said so, but I could tell. She was as tall as you, and had jet-black hair like you, too. It sat stiffly on her head like a dark beehive helmet. She could have been scary-looking, but she was my kindergarten teacher, my first teacher, and she was really, really nice.

Mrs. Smith sparkled as she moved through our classroom, the clicking of her high-heel shoes making her faster and taller; her polka-dot dresses lighting her cheery way. But the very best thing of all about her was the bright red lipstick she wore to school. Every single day. Her words were made funnier and smarter by the red lips they passed through.

I loved her.

She was loud. Even when she'd whisper, we'd hear her laugh clear across the classroom—but the way she laughed made us a part of the joke. Oh, and story time. Her eyes open wide, living inside the story, she took us there: "and *then* they all *ran* home, just as *fast* as their *stumpy little legs* would carry them!" Her red lips smiled, softening her booming voice.

I loved our noisy classroom, Mama, so different from home.

The next best thing was nap time. We took naps every day, toward the end of class. We each brought a special blanket to school just for nap time.

Mine was that beach towel you bought me, the one with big pink and orange flowers.

Our blankets stayed in their special spots in the cubbies. When it was time, we'd unfold them onto the floor, making a circle around the room. With our towels just touching at the top corners of the circle, we'd lay down with our heads pointing into the center.

I'd put mine next to my friend, Virgie. Virgie didn't live in town. She lived on the reservation with her family, a long bus ride away. She missed the bus a lot. She was gone to family ceremonies too, with her big family. She called the big family a clan, and the ceremony a sing. It could go on for days. The sing was often to help a sick person get well. When she came back, she smelled of cedar smoke from the wood fires they burned during the sing, like our fires when we went camping.

Virgie had long pretty black hair and laughed a lot, and when she did, her smile was as big as her face. She could run faster than me, too, even though she was shorter. At recess we would race to the monkey bars, and the first one there got to go first. Virgie started us most of the time. I wanted to go play at her house, feed her horses and sheep, but Mama said it was too far, too hard to get to. It was true that there wasn't a phone at Virgie's house.

Or a shower, either. They kept water in a big tank outside.

Once we all were lying down on our napping blankets, we'd start to quiet down. Virgie would giggle and I would too, turning to poke her in the side. "Stop it!" she'd say, laughing harder. Mrs. Smith turned off all the lights in the room. Everyone got quiet. Sometimes I would fall asleep.

The room got very still. Soon Mrs. Smith would put on her sparkly cape and her giant, glittery fairy princess crown, and pick up her magic wand. Humming softly, she'd walk around the darkened room. Passing by each blanket, her crown shining in the afternoon light streaming through the windows, she'd tap each of us lightly on the head.

Our fairy teacher with a crown, wearing her polka-dot dress and cape, magically awakened us.

"Wake up, wake up, dear children! Time to get up again!" she'd sing, in a song she made up for us each day. Soon the classroom lights came on. Yawning, I'd roll over, poking Virgie in the side again. Giggling, we'd get up, pulling our blankets from the floor with a shake. We'd fold them gently into their cubbies by our names, then sit down at our desks for quiet time reading practice. Soon the final bell would ring.

When it was time to go, I'd slow down at my desk as I put my sweater on. My house was a different kind of quiet from nap time here with Mrs. Smith, with Virgie and everyone.

Kids shouted goodbyes to one another. I found my lunch pail, the last one on the shelf, and waved to Mrs. Smith as the classroom emptied. Smiling broadly through red lipstick, she'd wave back, her brown eyes dancing, her teeth shining. My eyes and my whole face would smile back at her.

Then I'd be out the door, on the long walk toward home, and to you, Mama.

CHAPTER 18

Mrs. Zirker's Beauty Salon

"Come on, girls. We have to go now."

My sister and I unlock our eyes from the television and look at each other, wordlessly laying down our dolls. Turning it off, we leave the coyote and roadrunner to their cliffs and cactus highways and silently slip our shoes on. Heads bowed, we follow Mama out the door and climb into the plastic-covered back seat of the blue Buick Electra we call "The Boat," already warm from the Saturday morning sun.

We're going with Mama to see Mrs. Zirker, who'll cut and dye Mama's hair. We never want to go, but every few weeks, we have to anyway. At least there are lots of magazines. Mama hates driving, and we hate driving with her. Still, she needs to get her hair done.

"Going to get your fuzz fixed tomorrow? She did a job on you with her hairdryer last time. Your hair stood up like someone scared you!" Daddy says, with a howl of laughter at the dinner table the night before.

"That's not funny at all," Mama says, looking

at him, sighing, then dropping her head to stare at her empty plate. Daddy's jokes could be mean. His laughter made you jump or look away. It didn't make you laugh. You could be next.

The big car roars awake as Mama turns the key. Backing out of the driveway, it lurches violently to a stop again and again as she slams on the brakes, throwing us against the front seat and then the back, our arms whacking each other like pinballs. A neighbor and her dog stare at us from the safety of the sidewalk. Finally, Mama cranks the steering wheel, gunning the car forward, down the street. The neighbor starts walking again. The dog is still watching us, though.

Gliding to a stop, we park The Boat in front of the building and roll the windows up. My sister runs ahead and holds open the door to the beauty salon, slamming us into a wall of smell. The scent of sharp and sweet hair chemicals fills our noses and hangs in wild air buzzing loudly with hair dryers.

Mrs. Zirker is helping a woman out from under a hair dryer when she spots us across the room. "Hello! Good to see you! Be right there!" she shouts. Mrs. Zirker, the only beautician in town, is always busy.

"Thank you," Mama mouths back as Sandi and I spot chairs against the wall, silently deciding if we're going to race to them or not.

We've just settled peacefully into our chosen chairs—surprised we didn't want the same one—when Mrs. Zirker yells, "Come on over, I'm ready for you." She points to a chair for Mama. "Hi, girls!"

I raise my arm and wave limply back. I know what I'm in for.

Mama moves to the chair, and we leave our own and race to a large table stacked with fashion magazines. Mama thinks they're silly, which makes us like them even more.

"Those women look goofy. I can't believe anyone would spend money on those clothes, or makeup, or whatever it is. Imagine," she's said, and we do imagine, and like it all. I pick up a magazine and open it to pages of smiling women in short skirts and hair sticking up high, towering over raccoon eyes.

Now an hour has passed, and even the magazines hang limply off the table, spilling listlessly onto the floor. The hard chairs are solid rock now and have shrunk down even smaller beneath us.

"Mama? Can we walk outside? I'm tired," I moan, sneaking over to Mrs. Zirker's side.

"No. Absolutely not. Stay right here, right where I can see you," you say, raising an eyebrow under a cloud of shiny black hair goop, using your don't-ask-me-again tone. Sighing, I run off, flopping back down in my shrinking chair, kicking my feet against the wall underneath it in quick shotgun bursts, then moving to the one next to my sister.

"Don't sit by me!" she yells. "You're too wiggly! Go sit over there," she says, bossing me around, pointing to a chair clear across the room.

I roll my eyes at her, but get up and move there. No

one else is in these chairs at least, so I take the farthest chair and start humming.

Mama keeps chatting away with Mrs. Zirker, about S & H green stamps, and Daddy's work at the dam. Under the hair goop, she talks and talks, leaving us to busy ourselves as another hour passes.

Now I'm sitting on the floor, leaning against a wall, humming and smacking my shoes on the floor while my sister scowls at me across the room. Her fingers fly backward and forward through magazine pages she's already seen a thousand times.

Mrs. Zirker asks Mama to move to a chair by the sink where she can wash the goop out. It would be even longer before we'd leave. My sister looks at the clock, says that it's past lunchtime now, and we've been here since 10:00. Mrs. Zirker talks and talks, words flying out with each breath. How can she breathe and talk so much? Maybe she has gills like the fish in the lake. I decide she does. *Mrs. Zirker is a fish, glub, glub, glub....*

Mama, we have to come here with you all the time. It's like coyote jail, it's like falling off a cliff and slamming into the road below, and then you look up as a refrigerator lands right on your face.

~

Looking back, I imagine how it might have been that day, and on so many other days at the salon. I rewind the memory, and play it differently.

This time, we get up from watching cartoons to follow you to the car, but you stop at the front door. You say, "Girls, run and get your coloring books. Or your etch-a-sketch. We'll be there awhile." So, we do.

Once you're in the hair dye seat, you glance over and smile at us, your smile shinier than your goopy hair, and say, "You girls are so quiet. We've been here awhile, haven't we?"

We say, "Mama, we didn't eat breakfast, remember? And... I have to go to the bathroom really bad."

You say: "Oh, dear! Mrs. Zirker, can they use your restroom?"

"Of course! It's right that way, and it's open," she says, pointing down a hallway.

"I'm sorry, girls, I know it's hard coming, but you've been so good with your color books. You're too little to be home alone. Daddy had to work on the truck. How about we stop at the Pink Sands on the way home and get a hamburger and Coke? You girls were so quiet, I had no idea you were getting so tired."

The two of us sigh loudly. The Pink Sands! "Oh boy!" we yell, running for the bathroom. Mama looks at us tenderly, and shoots an imaginary, sweet smile after us.

~

But, here we are instead. Mrs. Zirker cuts and dries Mama's hair. I'm sitting on the floor in front of my sister, who doesn't look up. I'm spinning, spinning around, trying to kick her now, then spin and not kick her, then kick her again. She puts her head in her hands and softly cries. Mama's hair is dry. She gets up from the chair, walks to the counter and takes her checkbook out, while talking about casseroles with Mrs. Zirker. Mama whispers something, and Mrs. Zirker slaps her leg as they both laugh.

We run up to you, my sister's eyes pleading, like the coyote's eyes when he sees the big truck coming at him, but can't move before it smacks him.

Mrs. Zirker is saying, "Yack, yack, yack, well you just keep coloring your gray. You've got these two little girls here to look young for, yack yack, they're the perfect excuse!" You both smile and wave goodbye, and we trail out the door behind you to the car, unacknowledged, except as living, squirming proof you need to keep coming here, and we are forever doomed.

The mid-day sun burns down on us as we reach the car. My sister reaches to open the hot car door handle, using a corner of her shirt for a potholder. The heat inside blasts us like a blow torch. We want to roll down windows and air the car out before we get in, but your smiling Mrs. Zirker face is gone.

"Oh, stop whining. Get in right now. We're not going far," you snap, frowning under newly blackened hair. Mama starts the car, and it growls awake as she puts it in gear. Sandi and I sit on the hot dimpled plastic-covered seat, bare legs sizzling hot in our shorts, turning this way and that, eggs in a frying pan, as Mama grips the steering wheel hard, stares straight ahead, and drives us home.

CHAPTER 19

Canyon Country

Our town was built on a mesa, somewhere in the middle of the Colorado Plateau. The plateau is made up of layers of red rock sandstone, carved and shaped by rivers, rain, and eternal winds, and runs in all directions for hundreds of miles. There are no towns nearby. Hopi, Navajo, and Paiute people herded sheep and grew corn, beans, and squash here for centuries, scattered across shady canyons and cliff-built pueblos before the government decided to dam the Colorado River. They built a town here to help do that.

The government bought the canyon and the mesa from Navajo tribal people, swapping them for land further north. When I was in kindergarten, a Navajo boy in my class said his grandfather had owned that mesa, and his father before him; that it was given to them by a treaty. They grazed their sheep on thin, desert grasses up there, and grew crops down in Glen Canyon, on the fertile flood plains. Our town sits on Manson Mesa, named after my classmate's grandfather.

The government planned the town, then blasted

out a steep road to the top of the mesa and built it up there. The mesa itself sits a half mile from the shining, red-walled cliffs of Glen Canyon; the Colorado River roaring downstream, hundreds of feet below in the canyon bottom. A steel-arch bridge was built to span the canyon over the river, allowing people to cross over it easily for the first time ever. The dam sits right behind the bridge, holding back the deepening waters of the river, backing it up, and creating a lake as it fills up hundreds of miles of branching canyons.

The town was built for the workers building the bridge and the dam, like Daddy and most men in town, so they'd have real houses for their families to live in, unlike the old construction camp by the bridge site. The town was seven years old when we got here, and I started kindergarten. I'm in fifth grade now. There are twelve hundred of us—Navajo and Hopi people, government and Mormon families, looking outward from the mesa top to a colorful view of red rock cliffs that surround us.

It's a small town, but it's spread out, and covers the whole mesa. The streets are really wide. They curve around the mesa, and some still don't have any buildings. Out at the end of a still-gravel road to the east is a newly paved landing strip with a small trailer next to it. This is the airport. Navajo Drive sweeps to the west along the mesa edge, then south, facing the Colorado River, before it circles east, back toward the airport. The road is lined with churches there, the largest of them the Mormon Church, then the Catholic and Baptist Churches, followed by others. This is "Church Row." Daddy says the government built too many churches and bars, and that people spend too much time in one and then the other. Daddy says a lot of things like that.

Roads run in between the airport and Navajo Drive, both north-south and east-west, and in those wide streets lie the rest of the town, both the businesses and the houses. There is no mayor or town council. The town is run by the government. They hired teachers and built a school. They built one grocery store and hired a company to run it. Two doctors and a dentist were hired and a pharmacist to run the newly-built drug store. Two banks were constructed, as well as a small hospital. They built the beauty salon where Mama goes, and hired Mrs. Zirker to run it.

The store buildings are made of aluminum bolted to concrete floors. A small tree might be out front, half-buried in a gravel yard. When the wind gets blowing as it often does, the scraggly, larger trees in yards give up and fall over, surrendering their roots, and the aluminum buildings pull apart at the seams, and sometimes go flying like kites.

Nothing is old, or even wood or brick here—not like buildings in the city three hours south, where we drive to buy food. Down there, the hundred-year-old city is up higher, out of the desert heat and filled with green, fresh-smelling ponderosa pine trees. Houses come in all shapes and sizes, their yards thick with green grass; their window boxes bursting with petunias and pansies.

In our town, the government built houses out of concrete blocks, each one the same size as its neighbor, and painted them blue, orange, or gray. They own them and rent them to the men who work at the dam. Our house is blue, and one street away from the mesa rim.

Across the street from my house is an open red-sand desert, teeming with desert plants, lizards, and horny-toads—a place I love to explore.

Not everyone lives in a block house. Along Navajo Drive, the houses aren't concrete block but one-of-a-kind places where backyards face outward watching Glen Canyon and the lake. Business people who don't work at the dam live there, like the two doctors and the Mormon bishop's family. The boss of the whole dam has a house along there, too.

~

I had a friend who lived on that street. Her name was Jodi. We were best friends all year in third grade. We'd play kickball at recess, and run errands for our teacher, like picking up printouts for her at the office. One day late in the school year after I spent the night at Jodi's house, she wouldn't talk to me at school the next Monday.

"Jodi," I said, "let's eat our lunch at the bench next to the breezeway."

"Sorry, I can't," she said and walked away without another word. I sat alone, eating my baloney and mustard sandwich, pulling apart my Twinkie to eat the filling, licking my fingers, and wondering what was wrong. The next day was the same, and the next. The following week, when I came to school, her desk had been moved away from mine, across the room.

She started talking to the girl next to her like nothing had happened. It hurt so much that even Mama turned around one evening, looking at my sad face over the pile of dishes in the kitchen, and asked what was wrong.

"Jodi won't talk to me, and I don't know why. Maybe I did something." Mama told Daddy.

Daddy came to find me in my bedroom. "Well, my bet says it's because your friend is Mormon, and you aren't. They stick to their own. Her parents probably told her to make other friends at church. I wouldn't count on it changing. But you didn't do anything."

Daddy walked back into the kitchen, where Mama was still at the sink. "Jesus Christ! These people will be the death of me! It's the same shit down at the dam!" he bellowed to Mama, over the sound of running water.

Mama stopped, pursed her lips together, and shook her head. "It's rotten. They're just little kids," she said.

I could hardly believe what I heard, sticking my head around the laundry room wall, but I heard it. I was confused—I lost a friend, but somehow Daddy and Mama *were angry at Jodi's parents, and not at me.* The water just kept running over the dishes, though.

I cried myself to sleep that night, kicking the mattress above my bunk bed, which happened to be where Sandi was trying to sleep.

"Cut it out!" she yelled. "What's wrong with you? That hurts!"

"Sorry! But Jodi doesn't like me anymore," I moaned.

"Really? What happened?"

"I dunno. I spent the night at her house, we made popcorn and watched TV. Now she's not talking to me. Daddy says it's because she's Mormon and I'm not. Maybe her parents forgot until I was over there."

"Yeah, I know how that one goes," my sister sighed. She was in seventh grade, and seemed to know something more about Mormons and friends, but said nothing, and we soon fell asleep.

It was true Jodi had seven brothers and sisters, but I had three, although only Sandi and I lived at home now. But Jodi's house was big, with lots of kids and bedrooms. It had a wide green yard too, all one story, spread out along that last street of bigger houses, that looked out over the mesa's edge.

Her dad was the Mormon bishop.

~

Further up Navajo Drive, the nice houses stopped, and small pinkish trailer-type houses appeared. These had tiny, weedy patches for yards and fences made from chicken wire that leaned crookedly into the sandy wind. Navajo families lived here, although a few who worked at the dam lived in the concrete blockhouses. Mostly, though, they lived far from town, deep on reservation land. It ran north and west of our town and two hundred miles south, and even further to the east.

Apartment buildings and mobile home parks sprung up across the mesa toward the airport. The apartments had dry, sandy yards with chain-link fences. The mobile homes were all skinny, aluminum boxes shaped like matchsticks on wheels that sat back on bare spots of land, seemingly ready to roll elsewhere. It didn't feel like they wanted to stay there, and many of them were empty. I'd ride my bike through there, but I didn't stay long. People living in these areas didn't stick around long either after the bridge and dam were built. We stayed because Daddy helped run the new dam.

Daddy had a lot of thoughts about the town and people and shared these thoughts freely. He called some people who live here "real wild west characters" or "rough around the edges." Many came, he said, to hide out for a while from what they'd done or how they lived, because no one would think to look for them here. These characters were seldom seen in town. They blended in with the canyons and blowing tumbleweeds.

A few townspeople from Mormon pioneer families were related to families in a village ninety miles north of us, where a small group of Mormons with many wives lived with their many children. We drove by the turnoff to their canyon village on day trips, and Daddy pointed it out, but we never drove in. "Even the regular Mormons in town don't want much to do with these folks. Most Mormons gave up their extra wives or moved with them to Mexico. The government told them they had to if they wanted their territory to be a state. But some didn't, and there's a branch of them here."

When the villagers came to town, they dressed in old-fashioned prairie-type clothes, with bib aprons and bonnets. We saw them often in the stores, but they didn't talk to me or my friends when we saw them, and the kids didn't go to school here. Nobody mentioned the extra wives.

Unless you were related to the few pioneer families, people didn't move to town because they were from around here. The stubborn wind blew red sand into everything, after all. And everything cost a lot, especially food. People mostly came to work for the government, like Daddy. The government paid people good money.

The highways were wide and empty here. The closest town, a Mormon pioneer town, was eighty miles north, off of Navajo reservation land. It used to be a fort, to protect the pioneers against the local Paiute tribe, whose ancestral lands the pioneers were building their homes on. Before the government built the bridge across Glen Canyon, you couldn't get to that town without driving hundreds of miles, skirting the Colorado Plateau, to a narrow bridge, wide enough for two cars to scrape by, as the bridge rattled itself over the Colorado. This drive took all day.

The city to the south was a three-hour drive through wide open space—wild jagged cliffs, lizards, and sagebrush. People called it "Canyon Country," all part of the Colorado Plateau. There were side canyons in the cliffs, with lots of old ruins. It was vast and colorful, but a lonesome country, too. Mr. Llewellyn had pointed out in our history class that our town was too new to be on the state map.

"It'll be right about here when the new maps come out," he said, pointing to a little yellow box that read: "most remote area in the continental United States." That was true for me, but the Hopi people said their ancestors built those old ruins a long time ago, high up in the canyon walls. They weren't new people here, so they always knew right where they were.

Every month had a grocery day. We'd take the highway south to buy food, passing through Navajo country, dotted with tiny fields of corn, and hogans built of sticks and mud. This road took clear eyes and steady hands to drive it. Twenty miles south at The Cut, drivers came upon towering cliffs that seemed to be a dead end, until close-up, the cliffs parted, letting the narrow road pass through.

The Cut had been blasted through the two-thousand-foot jagged rock mountain, part of the Vermilion Cliffs range, and the road crept through it, opening suddenly to a vast, sweeping view of empty space bordered across a wide, flat valley. The space was framed by the many shades of red of the Vermilion Cliffs as they swept around the valley, highlighting the dark canyon in the middle, where the Colorado River streamed into the opening mouth of the Grand Canyon.

The road dropped down to the valley floor on the other side of The Cut. It was steep and long. Cars burned up their brakes driving down. They overheated coming up. The roadside was littered with them—hoods up, steam spilling into the air, or sitting, letting their brakes cool, the smell of scorched rubber rolling off the tires.

Once we reached the valley floor, we'd often be stopped by Navajo men on horseback, their shaggy-coated sheep flowing onto the roadway across the wide expanse of the scrubby desert plain. Daddy would smack the steering wheel and swear when he had to pull over, but I loved the bleating sheep, their voices filling the air with wild sounds, their hooves stirring up clouds of pink dust.

Riders on horseback with herd dogs led hundreds of them safely across, but for a time, our car was swallowed up, surrounded by a living river of animals, noise, and dust.

As the last sheep crossed over, Daddy would start the car, pulling back onto the dusty highway. Two long hours later, we'd reach the huge Safeway store where Mama shopped. Once we made the trek back home under darkening skies, Sandi and I would help move the month's supply of milk, bread and meat into the large freezer in the garage. It was a very long day.

~

The Navajo people struggled. They drove to town on weekends, buying over-priced goods at the stores, and washing clothes at the laundromats. Many didn't have plumbed water for kitchens or bathrooms, or electricity in their homes, and grocery stores on the huge reservation were scarce. The town knew that hundreds of people from the reservation would flood the small town on weekends, their dusty trucks filling the grocery store and laundromat parking lots.

Some of the Navajo men had taken to drink. Often we'd see a man sleeping in the doorway of a store, or back around the side of the building by the trash cans. It startled me to see a person that way, and I was uneasy walking around them to go inside the store, but I did. We all did. The struggle of the Navajo men seemed both invisible and overwhelming. It was always just there. Sometimes Mama wouldn't let us walk the few blocks alone to downtown on the weekends. There were a lot of fights around town, and stories, too of teenage boys picking on the sleeping men. A lot of car accidents happened then, too.

~

Native kids from the Navajo, Hopi, or Paiute tribes made up the biggest group in school. Some of my Navajo classmates only learned English—very different from their Native language—when they started school. The Navajo and Hopi kids also rode school buses from far away parts of the reservation, some even further than The Cut. The group of government and Mormon kids in class was often smaller than the Native kids.

The Navajo women dressed in beautiful clothing when they came to town to sell their turquoise and silver jewelry or the rugs they'd woven from their sheep's wool. Their velvet long-sleeve tops were often covered in handmade silver buttons that had been hammered down from dimes. The long, satin skirts they wore draped almost to the ground. They wore turquoise and silver bracelets and finely-made squash blossom necklaces with silver beads that jingled and sparkled in the sun. Long black hair was wound up neatly into a bun, with white cord holding it in place.

Mama loved their jewelry and rugs and saved up money to buy both. Symbols that were special to them and told stories about their view of the world were in everything they made. Once in awhile, she'd point this out to me and Sandi.

"Look!" She'd just picked up a Navajo rug that'd been on layaway for a while. "That square, jagged shape in the rug corner is a mountain, and there's one at each corner. And there's a lightning bolt that comes down each side. See? It's a Storm Pattern rug. The storm brings rain for the corn. And look here, this jagged shape is a water bug, showing how important water is in the desert." Mama could surprise me this way. She enjoyed decoding the meaning of their symbols like it was a puzzle. She had a book with pictures that showed types of jewelry and rug patterns, and native plants they could use for dye to color their wool.

These treasures were made by the same families struggling with alcohol. I thought something awful must have happened to them, but didn't understand it, unless it was because they sold their land so the dam could be built, and couldn't graze their sheep in the water-drowned canyons anymore. Much later, school library books like *Laughing Boy* by Oliver LaFarge taught me more about their history, but it wasn't in my school books.

The Hopi people too had a reservation, but it was further away, so many Hopi kids went to schools in distant towns. Many Hopi families still lived in their pueblos on the mesas southeast of us. Many beautiful types of artwork also flowed from their culture, including kachinas—wild-eyed colorful statues carved from cottonwood, and dressed up in paint, beads, leather, and feathers. There were different kachinas, each with a special power, like bringing rain or good health. Mama bought these too when she could, bringing them home and arranging them in a different order on top of the bookcase—the mud head dancer here, the eagle dancer there, then changing them up again. With each change, they seemed to tell a different story. And for the Hopi, that was true—the kachinas were doll-gods, who made the world go on through their dancing.

People in my town mostly talked about damming the river, and not the tribal cultures or problems around us. My life moved between the towns and the reservations, though, with school friends who lived out there or by traveling through to the grocery store or because our basketball teams played the Navajo teams at the distant boarding schools, and the middle school band, including me, went along.

I played the clarinet in the band and traveled where the band went. We'd bump along in the school bus over unpaved, dusty reservation roads. The schools, gyms, and outdoor fields had missing hoop nets and bleachers that needed painting. The schoolrooms where we'd warm up before playing had dusty older desks and cracked windows. They didn't look like ours.

Worst of all, these schools were boarding schools, which meant the school kids lived there, away from their families. My friend Virgie said her parents didn't want her to go there, because the kids got in trouble for speaking Navajo. It wasn't allowed. And she'd be far from her family. They let her take the long school bus ride from their house to school instead. We'd been friends since kindergarten.

People in town didn't seem to know that the kids at the distant boarding schools couldn't speak their own language, or how lonely that must be, living away from parents and brothers and sisters. They didn't see the sad shape of the schools, either, although our teachers who traveled with us did. I'd see them talking together when we visited, shaking their heads about it. Nothing ever changed in the years that I was there, as far as I could see.

CHAPTER 20

Mrs. Doland's Gift Shop

A ceramic cookie jar that used to be Mama's sits in my house now. Half hidden by a cabinet, it watches down over the kitchen from a shelf on the wall. Red roses encircle its square shape, flowing over and through a beige woven basket pattern. The lid lifts off the square jar by a single large, red rose. It was beautiful to my eleven-year-old eyes when I first saw it sitting on a shelf at Doland's Gifts. I smiled at the jar in that moment: you loved roses. I would get this for you. You would be so happy!

I bought it for Mama fifty years ago for Mother's Day, saving nickels, dimes, and quarters I earned from extra chores. I was old enough to babysit young children for a few hours, and Daddy paid me to stack wood and vacuum his shop. He knew I was saving money to buy you something.

"What do you need money for now? What kind of jar?" With a bottle of wood glue in his hands, Daddy stopped and looked curiously at me.

"It's a cookie jar. It's for Mama, for Mother's Day."

"Okay, kid. I'll pay you a buck fifty to clean up here when I'm done."

It took a long time to save for the cookie jar.

My friend Tina and I had found the pretty jar one day while I was walking her home from our house. We liked to stop at Doland's and wander through the aisles to see what was new, especially the aisle with art supplies. We'd found rainbow-colored pen sets, colored notepaper, and calligraphy pens there. Tina liked to buy pens and paper when she had money. She'd write notes on colored paper, and practice signing her name in the colored ink.

Today, she had enough to buy something.

"Look what I found! I have enough to buy both of these," she said, her eyes shining, picking up the purple pens and purple paper. "And guess what?"

"Tell me! What?"

"We can use it for the secret blood sister ceremony we're going to do. I'll write our oath on it! It'll be way better than Jodi and Jeannie's. Theirs was dumb. Jeannie showed it to me. Plus ours will be a secret, and be on this purple paper."

"Yeah! Cool!"

We walked through the rest of the aisles, stopping, suddenly, in front of the cookie jar. We loved the delicate jar, but my heart sank when I saw the price tag. It cost a lot. They'd sell it before I had enough money to buy it. We hurried back to the counter, and as Tina set her new pens and paper down, I asked Mrs. Doland how much I needed to put it on layaway.

"Oh, we require one-fourth down." She reached into her blue apron, pulled out a calculator, and set it on the counter. Her jaw firm, she punched in some numbers. "It comes to $4.50 down. Do you have that much?" Mrs. Doland peered over her glasses at me as I shook my head.

"No! But I can get it soon! Can you save it for me until then? For maybe two weeks?"

"No, I can't do that, but drop back in when you're close, and I'll keep an eye on it if it's still here."

Two weeks later, following long weekends of babysitting, I had the down payment, so Tina and I stopped in the following day. We ran to the aisle where we'd seen it. Turning the corner, my anxious gaze searched the shelves. I didn't see it. Oh, no! Wait—there it was! Still sitting up high on a display shelf, toward the back. It had been moved.

"It's here!" Tina let out a whoop.

"Yes, it's still here, girls!" Mrs. Doland stood smiling behind us. "I sat it up higher, thinking folks wouldn't notice it so much. I was pretty sure you'd come for it. You were so taken by it. It is nice. I think it was made in Mexico."

I brought it to the front counter and, carefully setting it down, danced around excitedly as Mrs. Doland wrote up the layaway ticket. She taped it to the front of the cookie jar, handed me a copy, and carried the jar to the back, setting it on the layaway shelf. It was safe now. No one could buy it, and I had plenty of time to pay it off.

~

I spent the night with Tina the following weekend. She wrote and rewrote the words to the blood sister oath on scratch paper until she was satisfied. Then she wrote it out, line by line, on the purple paper, in purple ink. She drew lines for us to sign, and wrote our names in neatly below them.

I brought a needle from Mama's sewing chest so we could prick our fingers. Later that night, we got up, and Tina closed her bedroom door and drew the curtains. We lit a candle. We recited the oath to each other as the candle flickered, twisting shadows across the dark bedroom walls and curtains.

"... and if I tell anyone I am your secret blood sister, I'll die and rot away from this cruel world..."

We signed our names in purple ink. Poking my finger, I winced, then squeezed it until a tiny drop of blood appeared. I made a red smeary dot next to my name, and Tina did the same.

"Friends forever and ever, right?"

"Right! Forever and ever. Until we're dead!"

~

Months passed after that night. I'd been stopping into Doland's, making payments every two weeks. The day finally came when I had enough saved to pay it off. Mother's Day was still almost a month away. Tina and I walked up to the counter that last time, and I handed Mrs. Doland the final three dollars. She looked at me, her face bright as she came back from the lay-away shelf with the jar. She stamped her ticket *Paid In Full*, and handed it to me.

"What a beautiful present for your mother! She'll love it. You've worked hard."

"Yeah! And now I can give it to her." Mrs. Doland wrapped it in brown paper, and put it in a small cardboard box to make it easier to carry home. I said goodbye to Tina as she walked off toward home. I turned the other way, holding the box close for many blocks until I reached our house.

Looking around to be sure no one saw me, I snuck inside the front door and tip-toed down the hall into my bedroom. I needed a good hiding place where Mama wouldn't find it, but at least it was wrapped in brown paper. Mama had a habit of poking around in my things; opening drawers, digging through my books, and even opening them to read notes from friends that I'd hidden there. I didn't like it, but didn't know what to do. I sat the jar on a shelf in my closet next to the wall. I'd keep moving it to keep ahead of Mama's searching. I was sure there wasn't much in my bedroom that Mama missed.

The day was almost here! Sandi and I paid Daddy to buy a cake mix, powdered sugar, and food coloring to bake the cake, the day before the holiday. We hurried around the kitchen that morning, my silent sister and I, gathering mixing bowls and spoons and shuttling them into Daddy's shop next to the garage. Mama wouldn't hear the mixer running, and Daddy was in the backyard. We turned the oven to the right temperature, glancing out the living room window and up the street, hoping her car wouldn't pull in from her trip to the store.

"There's her car! She's turning into the driveway. Hurry!" I raced to the oven, potholders ready, and grabbed the cake. Sandi flung open the door to the shop and closed it behind me. Seconds later, Mama came through the front door. The whole house was filled with a sugary-sweet smell she surely must have noticed, but nothing was said.

This was a good kind of silence. And later too, as I closed my bedroom door, hoping I wouldn't hear her steps coming down the hallway while I was wrapping the gift, I didn't. The silence of the space held. I took this as approval for what she surely knew was going on.

I pulled the cookie jar out from its final hiding place under the bed and unwound Mrs. Doland's plain brown paper. Placing it carefully on a sheet of shiny gold birthday paper, I pulled the paper up around the uneven sides of the jar and taped it to the top of the rose. I turned it, pulled the paper up, and taped it until the whole jar was inside the paper. I added curling ribbon with all the skill my eleven year-old self could muster. I was ready.

The next morning on Mother's Day, we brought in the cake and presents while Mama waited in the living room.

Daddy was out in the garage. "No, I can't stop,

girls. I'm busy. Go ahead without me."

Sandi had bought and wrapped Mama a new mixing spoon, and set it on the kitchen table, next to my gift and the cake. "We're ready! You can come in now!"

Mama walked in, still in her blue zip-up robe, and sat down at the table. Her face a blank, she moved toward the table, and quickly opened Sandi's gift. Her head seemed to move in a nod. Then she pulled my wrapped gift over until it was right in front of her.

She opened it slowly, glancing at it, then past it, to something outside the window, something outside of our lives, then suddenly back to me, my sister, and the table. Her eyes back on the gift, I held my breath, as her eyes lingered on spots with too much tape; her fingers running over the top of the package, bulky with unevenly cut paper. She frowned—finally pulling out the cookie jar.

"Huh. Well, that's nice," she said, her eyes moving to the lopsided cake, its icing littered with cake crumbs. My heart fell. I watched her, my eyes filling with tears, willing her to say more. Sandi looked at Mama, then at me, but said nothing. She looked down at the floor.

"We'll save the cake for dinner. You can set it on the counter. Thanks, girls."

Mama stood up, gathered up the wrapping paper, put it in the trash, and left the kitchen. I ran to my room and closed the door, shutting out Mama's silence that echoed through the house, through my bedroom walls. Throwing myself across my bed, tears spilled over, finally, for everything that hurt, for everything I didn't understand.

~

So much silence, Mama. Whole parts of my childhood are an empty, blank space of what might have happened, but didn't. Nothing horrible, some might say, just a vacuum of space between a daughter's gift, and the mother who received it. In your dark silences I felt forgotten or bad.

The child I was kept trying to reach you, tried to find ways to make you smile. That child took up the cause of your happiness, not understanding the magnitude of what she'd chosen, not knowing there were other choices. There were intricate gifts that as a child, I made for you—framed embroidery, cross-stitched pillows, paint-by-number paintings. There were gifts I saved for and bought you, like the cookie jar.

Years later, when my life widened, I brought you gifts from my travels to other countries, where what I witnessed broadened my understanding of what parents and family life could be. Cultures and families were often intertwined, with kids helping parents in a family store, or sometimes working together on their small farm, throughout the day. Where temple monks visited with families, where lush, nurturing landscape itself seemed to wrap around me, around the villages and families in an easy, familiar way. Kids walked with their parents at night, chatting with neighbors along the way to a celebration or church or temple. These cultures seemed vastly different than what I'd known at home.

Spiritual teachings in the many temples where I

meditated cultivated a broader kindness toward others, toward you, and toward myself. I shared this generosity of spirit I was finding. I brought you a silk robe from Thailand, pottery from Mexico, woven shawls from Tibet, and textiles from India, all carefully chosen by me during traveling pilgrimages. These were received by you, your face brightening in surprise like the warmest sunset, but only for that brief moment before the sun falls below the horizon and the earth darkens again. With that darkening, my gift was set aside, exiled that same day or the next to an airless drawer or a dark closet. I was still that child who gave you useless gifts.

~

That child grew through the ten thousand losses she could never grasp, somehow finding a way; those agonizing years of becoming are much more behind me than before me. That child I was still lives in me, Mama, and is still growing. And in the now-sweetness of my daily life, I am often, simply, happy. Once in a while, that cookie jar with the rose-handled lid draws my gaze up to it. It came back to me in that slow, circle dance of years—became mine once again—after you died.

And in that moment when I look up, I see how pretty it is, the same as when Tina and I first saw it at Mrs. Doland's so long ago. Then I smile, remembering that night of the blood sister ceremony. How Tina and I are still friends; how I still have that oath written on purple paper, stashed safely away in a drawer of my jewelry chest.

And then I think of you, Mama.

CHAPTER 21

A Billion Stars and Eyes and Seeing

The stars blossom in darkness like white flowers. Crystal flowers that sparkle dimly or brightly, unless you look straight at them. Then the pale ones hide from you. If you look away, then sideways, you'll see them all again. But there are so many stars, so many, that the shy, dim ones don't matter. They'll come out brighter when it's darker; when they're ready.

Or maybe they're hiding. It's okay to hide. It's good to know how.

The whole night sky is a giant eye, peering down as I look up at it, watching it shine through star flowers that twinkle and dance. It's bigger than the desert, and the desert is everywhere. But the sky, oh the night sky! It's as dark tonight as I've ever seen it be. I bet it's blacker tonight than the bottom of the ocean.

Then, there's a falling star. There it goes! — a bottle rocket leaving a trail of shimmers your eyes follow until you can't see it anymore, but you keep looking to get that feeling back of first seeing it. There's the Big Dipper, too; I see it after spotting the one bright star in the handle. We lay here, both of us quiet tonight, my sister and I, on the blanket spread out in the back yard, on this hot summer night, swatting mosquitoes and watching stars.

Now, there's a satellite. Here's how you find a satellite. I taught Tina, too. You look at the sky, but keep your eyes loose and blurry, like you're seeing everything but not holding it tightly in front of you. You hold your head still. You wait. Then, something up there moves a little. But stars don't move, unless they're shooting stars, and those are fast. Then you look again out of the corner of your eyes, like it's a shy star. It's not that bright, but you see it now, and yes, it is moving.

"Look! It's a satellite!" I pointed toward it.

"Where?"

"Over here— hold your eyes still and keep looking."

My sister nods; she knows how to spot a satellite, too. "Oh, I see it! That's the second one. I saw the first one, though."

"So? I don't care." I get tired of being last. I'm eleven, and not so little.

"Let's look for the Milky Way."

We lay, flat on our backs, staring up. "Oh, there it is! I missed it before, but it's right over there!" she says, pointing up near the top of our only tree in the backyard.

"Oh, cool, I see it. Oh, wow! There's so many stars. It's like a path lit up across the sky. Virgie told me the Milky Way got made when Coyote threw a bag of stars at the sky, and they spilled loose everywhere."

"That can't be true! Your friend doesn't know everything."

"She said so. Her grandma told her."

We look into the face of this dark night sky with the milky path to somewhere, winking at us over our sleeping desert, and dream of satellites and coyotes with bags of stars. I fall asleep under its gaze. Then the screen door slams, and suddenly Mama is standing over us. She has on a denim shirt with flowers sewn onto it, but her face is dark. It could use some stars.

"What are you girls doing out here? It's late! Get inside and go to bed!"

So we do. But Daddy's already asleep, so we don't hurry. Mama doesn't know our secrets about how to see shy stars or find satellites. They're not really secrets, but you have to ask us how it works, you have to want to know. She doesn't.

We don't tell her, either.

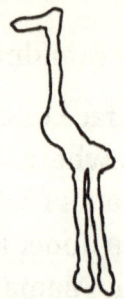

CHAPTER 22

Letting Go of Mama's House

I was surprised that Mama's house in the desert sold so quickly. Real estate had fallen in the rural area but crept back up in the last few years. The house was still a tribute to the 1970s, when it had been finished and first occupied. Prior to that, Mama and Daddy had spent long weekends for years, doing what building they could manage, alongside the contractors.

The house was small but sound, with a clear mortgage. A full-grown magnolia tree had long stood out front, and a huge maple tree spread its shady branches across the side yard. Mama and Daddy had planted both of them as young saplings. The yard and garden areas were thriving. The old grape vines Daddy had planted before the house was even built were neglected now, but still growing. I was sad to see the property go, but it needed new owners, new stories. And it was worth more than I'd expected. Mama had taken good care of it for forty years, after all.

Much of the furniture and household items had been sold in an estate sale, and Sandi, Donna, and I had peacefully divided up Mama's collection of Native American art and jewelry. Her art blended with my own, purchased over the decades of growing up and living in the Southwest. Each of my pieces told a timely story about my adult life, and Mama's small collection added stories from our early family years.

After the memorial service, Donna retreated back into her life centered around work as a hospital nurse. Sandi and I met down at Mama's house one last time before the sale was completed, to move out pieces of furniture we wanted to keep, and drive them to our homes in other states.

Sandi was arriving today, but I was already at the house, and spent an evening flipping through Mama's many books that were still on the shelves. I noticed how many I'd bought her across time. Books like Jack Kornfield's *A Path With Heart*, about the Theravada Buddhist tradition I was deeply involved in then. A photography book on Tibetan Buddhism sat next to it, and next to that was a book on the life of the Hindu sage Ramana Maharshi. I could trace my inner evolution by looking at the books I'd given her over a span of many years. There was also a book I'd given her on Guatemalan weaving, because of her interest in Navajo rugs. She had been a constant reader and encouraged me, too, and I'd always hoped we might talk through books if not spoken words.

Many of the other books, such as Mark Reisner's *Cadillac Desert*, and Russell Martin's *A Story That Stands Like A Dam* were about the building of Glen Canyon Dam, and its impact on local Native American tribes and wildlife, both above and below the dam. She never mentioned any of these books to me, although she thanked me for each one, and put her *"Personal Library Of:"* sticker on the front page of most of them. I assumed, perhaps wrongly, that she never read any of them. I never did know.

~

"I'm on the hill by the creek! See you in a sec," Sandi said from her cell phone. Moments later, the sound of a car engine followed by a door slamming in the driveway brought me outside to greet my sister. I gave her a hug and wheeled her suitcase into the house.

"That's *such* a long drive! I covered four hundred miles today." Her face looked tired, and she shivered in the cool afternoon sun with only a tank top and capris on. She walked to the kitchen sink and filled a glass with water, drank it, refilled it, and brought it into the living room, collapsing onto the only chair besides the loveseat.

"It's so weird to be here. I've been thinking about it all the way down, wondering what it'd be like in the house, without her here."

"Yeah, I felt that way when I got in yesterday."

Sandi set her empty water glass down on the carpet next to her chair. "Mama was who she was. But whenever

I came here, she was glad to see me. She loved to cook for me, and I loved her *to* cook for me, so that worked fine for a few days." She fell silent on the chair.

I nodded. "It's been nice being here in the house. Although part of me feels almost like Mama's going to pop in here any second, and tell me to go do something for her. The grown-up me *really* wishes we could keep the house. I'd need you to go in with me on it, though."

"Yeah, I can't do it. Too much money, too far away."

"Yeah, for me, too, I guess. I just hate selling it. I've been driving to, or flying down here to this place for forty years, and it's hard to let go." I looked around the room at the empty adobe brick walls, then through the living room window, at the tall cottonwoods along the creek across the street. "It's been even longer than that, Sandi. We came here as school kids; we helped them clear this land forty-five years ago. When they finally moved here, I came down a lot. Then I got divorced and ended up in New Mexico. I was a single mom, living on food stamps and all kinds of state-subsidized help for years. I went to college and then law school, and worked crazy hours at the legislature in Santa Fe. You'd been gone for years. Part of that time, we weren't talking."

"I remember. I missed a lot of years. And you were busy," Sandi said quietly.

"I was. But I was older, too, and tolerated Mama more. She was lonely after Daddy died. I drove over some weekends. Tried to keep her company. I still hoped she'd change, but by then she was in her late seventies. I was changing, though. We had a few things in common, like gardening and a love for local Native American culture. I liked to look through her collection of old family photos and copy them, and she'd tell me what she knew. Sometimes we'd go out for breakfast or lunch—before she quit talking. You know how that went." I looked at my sister, who nodded, her face shuttered.

"Yeah. I have too many of those stories myself." She sat in her chair, looking out the window.

"Time slowed down here, my busy life in Santa Fe got put on pause. Man, was that nice! Even when Mama wouldn't talk to me, she'd feed me. It was kind of freeing, after I'd learned to make peace with some pretty hurt feelings. Room and board with few expectations. Do you remember she cut out hiking articles for me, Sandi? She had a whole file."

"Yeah, I do. I saw it around here the last couple years or so."

"Me, too. After all this time. After she shut down, I'd switch to checking out the hikes or visiting ruins. It sounds odd, but maybe those were our best years. It could be sad or sort of boring, but okay enough at times, too. Then on one of my rambles, I found that wilderness area up the road. That was maybe fifteen years ago. Remember? The hike place with that old cattle trail, the creek with the swimming hole, and those crane petroglyphs."

Sandi nodded. "Yeah, I remember the first time I went there with you. Donna came too; we all went swimming. What a gorgeous spot."

"Yeah, it was. And it's still one of my favorite places here. I felt more at home after I found that place. I liked being out there about as much as visiting our mother. It's all a part of what's been here for me, Sandi. It's like the Cliffs when I was a kid. It's still here, without Mama or the house."

Sandi shifted in her chair and looked thoughtful, but was silent for a while. "Yeah. I'll miss it all, too. But I wasn't here very much like you were, and didn't stay long, when I was. I moved away after high school and was just mad about pretty much everything she did and didn't do. I didn't feel like coming down much to see her, except for her birthday, when we all were here.

"When you and I really dug in and patched things up between us, that changed a lot for me. But it wasn't that long ago, and I didn't come more often. We talked it out after Lynn died, so maybe ten years ago?"

"Yeah, that's about right. Maybe eleven." I tried to calculate the years, then gave up. "Not sure, Sandi."

"That's okay. But it's true that after that, it was more fun to come. Being around Mama was a little easier with everyone here."

Sandi paused and looked at her watch. "I'm getting pretty hungry. And I have a bottle of wine in the car for later, if we can find a couple of glasses."

"Ha, good! There's a few left. Let's go grab a bite to eat." Sandi sat up, stretching her arms overhead, and yawned.

"Oh, Sandi—I found a stack of photo albums in the bookcase. Let's flip through them before we start to pack up tomorrow."

"Good idea." Sandi took her glass over to the sink and sat it down. "Should I call Donna? Does she know we're here?"

"No, I haven't called her yet," I said. "Hmm... can we wait until morning? Then the evening won't get complicated. I don't know why she's still the way she is around me, but she is. I don't want to deal with it if she stops by later. I know it's about things Lynn said eons ago, but at this point, I don't know what's left of that. And she won't say."

"Yeah. I don't know, either. Okay, let's call tomorrow. What's in the photo albums? Are they early? Mama and Daddy in the Navy?"

"No, during the dam years, and building this house. Maybe a few in Indiana."

"Well, it's our last night for that stuff. Let's go find dinner first. I'm not driving, though!"

CHAPTER 23

The Cliffs: An Aliveness That Knows

We have to move when I'm in sixth grade. Not to another town, but to another house. I find out about a new government plan from Daddy one night at dinner.

"We're hearing that they're not going to rent the houses much longer. The government wants out of the running-a-town business; they want the place to have a mayor and town council. They'll keep running the dam, though. We're done with construction; we're making electricity these days."

"What? What are we supposed to do? How much

time do we have?" Mama asks, her voice rising.

"Oh, a year, maybe more. It won't happen fast. They'll put the houses up for sale, and everyone will have to buy the one they're renting, or find one they like better and grab it. Like a damn game of musical chairs."

"Alright. That's a relief. Well, that's huge news. It's going to shake the whole town up. At least we have some time." Mama frowned over her now empty dinner plate.

"Well, we're not buying this house. We're going to move someplace away from this goddamn blowing sand dune across the street," Daddy says.

"Are Donna and Lynn coming back to live with us in the new house?" I ask, worried this might happen, especially with Lynn the wolf.

"No, it'll stay just you two. Those girls are on their own. You'll keep your bedrooms."

I still don't like the idea of moving. Everyone I know, every friend I have on our street would be far away, or maybe, gone. How would I see my friend Donald, who lives next door? Soon I wouldn't be able to walk next door and knock, and wait for him to come out and play.

Daddy doesn't like it here, though, doesn't like the wild, open desert across the street, the place I hide inside, where plant and animal worlds call me closer, to look inside their lives. Theirs is a real world, like ours, but smaller. Like our bigger world, this one has rules; rules that can be hard, but are out in the open, clearer than the ones in my house. I'm at home with the lizards and the wild desert grasses that hide them, with the yucca and sagebrush that grow in the powdery, red sand.

When the wind blows, as it so often does, my desert wakes up, rubs its eyes, and comes alive. With help from the wind, that desert gets up and moves. Grain by grain, it flies through the air, dimming the sun and faraway cliffs. Flying low along the streets, the wind paints everything the color of sand. Tree leaves and branches tear off and sail away on the breeze. Leaves and branches left behind on trees are outlined in fine red sand. Lawns fill up and turn red, too.

The wind can funnel back on itself, too, making small tornadoes called sand devils. Sand devils can come after you, whipping your bare legs with needle-sharp sand, whacking you with sticks and tumbleweed prickles it's picked up on its shifty way. Turning and walking home backward in wind, and watching for sand devils is something I learned by first grade.

The wind helps the sand climb into my hair, and slide into my clothes, too. Then I wake up in the morning with a red, sandy pillow. It falls out of my ears and hair at night. Red sand lines my bedroom windowsill, coming through the tiniest of cracks. Mama cleans it up, but it comes right back.

I don't want to move. Doesn't the wind blow everywhere in town? And the houses are all built exactly the same too, except for the color. How could another house be better than ours?

We move anyway. To an orange house many streets away, a street with houses on both sides and no wild, drifting desert nearby. The new house sits next to a square, blue one on the corner. It has a bigger backyard, a willow tree down at the edge of the fence to climb, and a big, sunny spot for a garden for Daddy. A white, spicy-scented rose bush with long branches and dark green shiny leaves stands in front of a long trellis. The house is the same, but the yard is better. I miss my friend Donald, though, and don't see him anymore, because it's too far to walk, too confusing to find the way. A girl from my class, Sharon, lives right behind us now. Maybe we could be friends.

~

Our house is on the next-to-last street in town, and I soon find out what this means. A couple of weeks after we move in, I walk out the front door and around the block, to see if Sharon can play. We'd talked at school and decided I'd come by soon. But suddenly, my gaze is drawn up and out. Looking down the street, a wide-open vista meets my stare. An empty lot between two houses opens the view wider as I look, spreading out beyond the houses to miles and miles of mesas of all sizes and colors. Framed above by blue sky, an even bluer lake wanders distantly through it all. Mesas and sky and blue, as far as I can see.

I look over now toward Sharon's house and suddenly know I won't see her today, even though I'll be in trouble if Mama looks for me there. One foot and then the other steps off the sidewalk, taking me across the street toward that view. I walk up to the empty gravel lot and look around. No one is watching. I walk through it.

A barely visible, sandy trail appears on the other

side, picking up where the gravel stops. It leads toward the mesa's edge; toward the horizon. It invites me in, like Sharon's mother would if I were knocking at her door now. Instead, I'm following the soft call of this openness now before me. Stepping lightly onto the sandy trail, I let it guide me. It unfolds in a straight line for a while, and then twists and turns down to a stream, where water splashes out of a small culvert. Past there, it gurgles along, running freely to where silver-green tamarisk bushes grow frilly and tall, blooming pink at the edge of their branches. Cat tails and rushes line the water's edge, their brown heads bobbing slightly in the light breeze. The thirsty bushes drink the water, but still, it babbles through, moving on with the stream.

I follow it further, and the small stream slows and widens into puddles here and there, forming tiny, marshy ponds. A gentle smell I don't know—moist soil, growing plants, something wild—wafts up in the air to my nose, a smell of utter aliveness. An aliveness that tickles my nose, my ears, and eyes; it seems to hold many things, maybe everything. Enchanted by the scent of the air, I stop at a tiny pond's edge and bend down, startled by this marsh close to my house, which now seems far away. Like the dry, open desert that used to be across the street, there's another world here, both smaller and much, much wider. A wonder revealed itself after I stepped off the street, when I meet the horizon's gaze, and followed it to this rich aliveness.

Crouched on the muddy sand by the pond, I touch the water, and it springs to life beneath my fingers. Pollywogs! How could they be here in the desert? Yet, they are. Maybe they were led here, too, by that scent of earthiness in a desert. Slow-moving pollywogs show themselves as I swirl my fingers in the lukewarm water. Cupping my hands together, I catch a few and watch them wiggle in my palms. Some have two back legs. They seem half frog and half fish. I slide them softly back into the pond.

Unsure how much time has passed, I retrace my steps up the trail toward home, glancing over at Sharon's house as I cross the gravel onto the street. I won't tell her what I've found, I want it to be my secret for now. Coming back a few days later, I sit on the sand by the marsh all afternoon, watching pollywogs that now have four legs. A few days more and I find that most of the pollywogs have lost their tails, and are hiding at the water's edge or in the grasses, having hopped out of the marsh as the tiniest of frogs.

~

I squeeze all the time I can out of that summer, exploring the hidden desert wonderland I've found. I go to The Cliffs often, following the trail further down, around the mesa. Along the stream the following summer, new flowers bloom and new animal tracks appear— rockslides too. The small stream bubbles its way down the hill, trickling over the warm mottled pink and orange sandstone beyond the marsh, forming a tiny waterfall where the sloping edge of The Cliffs begin, dropping down at the mesa's edge.

I stop along that steepening side. Finding a flat spot, I lower myself down to lay on the warm sandstone beneath me. Stretching my arms out, my cheek rests on the sandstone, my palms softly resting on the warm, grainy earth. The curve of the cliff meets the side of my cheek, and all the way down into my belly and legs, the warmth of the sandstone lifts up and through me. A rush of love for these pinkish-brown cliffs, the very color of my skin, moves through me. Tears spring up from somewhere deep, spilling out of my eyes, darkening the sandstone. I rest with the cliff; its shape fits beneath me. I doze in the sun.

Soon I turn over to watch the sky until I feel like sitting up. Hidden at what feels like the end of the world, warm, pink sandstone slopes down in gently rippling layers, striped now in beige and pink, ending in hundreds of tiny lizard stairs that I can go down, too. Pink stairs of warm, pretty sandstone, with spots and tiny cracks where lizards might hide, but other desert dwellers might, too. I walk carefully, taking wide steps over these shaded places.

Further down from the trickling waterfall, smaller cliffs drop down and even out onto a wide sandstone bench. I see that round dips have been carved by water into the flat sandstone, leaving potholes behind. The holes are dry, with a sandy layer in the bottom. Some are wider and shallow; some are small but deep. I walk into one and sit down; it's like an empty bathtub.

A week later, there's a sudden rainstorm. Rain pours, flashes of lightning and booming thunder fill the air, and then—it's gone. I remember the holes, and slip out of the house the next day. I find them brimming with water. The ones near the shady cliff ledges are cold. The now-full holes reach out across the sandstone bench. A couple of small ones are warm already, like little swimming pools, with water up to my shins when I wade in.

In a few days, something tiny, almost invisible, swims away when I stick my hand in a larger pothole. Little swimmers I can barely see, swimmers with lots of legs. I lay down and put my face right to the water while I stick my hand in, and watch. They look a little like the sea monkeys in my science class last year. Fairy shrimp, as pinkish as the sandstone, and so clear you can almost see through them swim slowly; their many tiny legs fanning them forward as they glide about in the hole.

Little worlds come and go so quickly here. Two or three weeks later, I find the holes dry again. I don't know where the fairy shrimp came from or where they went. They must live a whole life in these short weeks. I run my fingers through the drying sand at the bottom of a hole, but there's nothing there. The desert is startling, it makes me smile to myself and to everything, to the sagebrush I stopped to look at on the trail down, full of baby caterpillars. I brush my hands off now, laughing as I get up, and twirl around, while the desert dreamily watches. Yes, the swimmers were real, I tell myself. I saw them. I touched them. And they're gone now.

Desert magic is everywhere, in the swirling colors of sandstone globes shaped by wind into giant ice cream cones; in the smell of the heavy air before it rains, and then after, when the sagebrush scents that same fresh air. Breezes move lightly over the desert grasses, an airwave that flows across the land, into the sea of the sky. Once when I saw this wind, the way it rippled so slightly over the plants made me swallow hard, even though I felt happy. I sat down and watched it from up high, dangling my legs off a ledge, my bare feet hanging, full of a tender happiness. I knew then I'd always be safe out here, that peace would be here waiting to take me in when I came back, especially when things were hard at home.

~

I grow bigger, and go further down The Cliffs as the summers pass. Tina comes with me now, and Sharon too. We pretend we live there. That our parents are gone away, that we're a tribe of girls. We hide food and clothes in the tamarisk bushes; we carve our names in the sandstone. We practice climbing barefoot down the sloping, grainy cliffs at the mesa edge. Finally one summer, we climb all the way down off the mesa with only our two bare hands and two bare feet, laughing, whooping with the sheer joy of it, of feeling the warm rock, of becoming like lizards.

On some afternoons, I go down along the path by myself, stashing my shoes in a tamarisk bush, then running barefoot down the trail. I'm there so much some summer weeks I seem to visit home only to eat and sleep. I sit down at the sandstone ledge past the little stream. Looking out into the face of the sprawling landscape, I watch the changing colors of the cliffs—beige, gray, rose to shades of purple—layered across the horizon like dominos laid sideways, one behind the other. Closer in, there's Glen Canyon Dam, with the tiny steel bridge in front. It looks like a toy from here, with little cars driving across. Further out is Cathedral Rock, shining over the main bay by the edge of the marina, with the miniature Park Service trailer park above it. Beyond, just before the edge of the skyline is the hand-like shape of Lone

Rock, right in the middle of the lake. It stands tall with its solemn white-gray cliffs shaped like a giant thumb and fingers, rising powerfully from the lake bottom.

I sit watching until Daddy gets off work, and from my ledge at the edge of the earth, I spot his little blue truck. Here it is now, far away, coming up the dam access road, onto the highway. There'll be trouble if I'm not home before he gets there, and big trouble if he and Mama find out I'm not at Sharon's house. I stand up and brush myself off as my heart begins to pound. I run like crazy, racing him home. I'm at the top of the trail, and I look back to see he's turned off the highway and is coming up the steep road onto the mesa. He'll be at our block and in our driveway quickly. I run faster, knowing he can't see me, racing up to the pavement, across the black asphalt street, around the sidewalk corner, and into our yard, my legs pumping, my lungs screaming for air. Down the street I see him turn the far corner, coming toward our house. He pulls into the driveway, seconds after I fall, sprawling onto the lawn, panting. Daddy gets out of his car and walks over to where I lay, breathing hard, flat on my back. He looks down, studying me.

"What's up, kid? Why're you so out of breath?"

"I'm just running from Sharon's, and I'm a little late, is all."

Daddy stands there, looking at me, then around the front yard, as if weighing this. "Well, go on in then, your Mama needs your help setting the table."

"Okay, Daddy."

"Tell her I'll be in the shop for a bit."

"Okay, Daddy."

Daddy walks off toward the garage door. I exhale, take a deep breath, and step inside, closing the door behind me.

CHAPTER 24

A Reckoning

Mama is waiting in the living room for me, though, when I come inside.

"Where've you been?" she asks, hands on her hips, her flowered denim shirt disguising her dark, angry thunderhead face.

"I was at Sharon's," I say, looking at my sandals. I want to tell her about the stream, about all of it, but I can't. I heard Daddy say to her that some boys fell down there awhile back and got hurt. He told her the cliffs were dangerous. But Mama wouldn't listen anyway, even if that wasn't so. I can't tell her.

"No, you weren't. Her mother was out in her backyard, and she said you weren't there. She hasn't seen you in days. Where were you? Go to your room! Now! Your dad will come and talk some sense into you."

I'm scared—I know what that really means about Daddy. It's not about talking. I walk down the hall to my room and look around, but there's nowhere to hide.

Soon enough, I hear the garage door by the shop slam, and then Mama's voice, low and angry. Then Daddy throws the bedroom door open, crashing it loudly into the wall behind it. His face is like Mama's, only the thunderhead has let loose into a storm.

"You've been lying to your Mama!" He closes the door behind him, taking off his belt. *Mama, why do you send him to do this? He does it to Sandi, too.*

After he leaves, I crawl under my bed and finally fall asleep, my stomach growling. I thrash around on the cold tile all night, the many tender spots aching. In the middle of the night, Sandi knocks on the wall between us. I don't knock back.

~

I still went to the Cliffs after this happened, Mama, but not as often. And I was careful not to stay as long. I still wanted to tell you why I went, but I didn't know why, myself. I knew what would happen if I was caught again. And yet, I went for years.

It was beautiful and free there. And I was beautiful and free there.

CHAPTER 25

Summer: Lake Time

There was a time when, in my search for essences, I concluded that the canyonland country has no heart. I was wrong. The canyonlands did have a heart, a living heart, and that heart was Glen Canyon and the golden, flowing Colorado River.
~Edward Abbey

If someone could see me from up above, looking down, this is what they'd see: stillness. And blueness. And the form of a girl in the middle of it all. Arms open, palms down, legs stretched out wide, my floating body is shaped like a star. Holding my breath and floating face down, the only sound I hear is the soft, lapping water surrounding and holding me. Hot summer sun—sun as hot as a meteor—burns my back, my legs, and my arms, while cool lake water covers the submerged front of my body. I feel hot and cool at the same time.

Suddenly waves hit my side, breaking over the back of my head. Choking, I stand up in chin-deep lake water and look toward where it came from. Cecily, my friend from school grins back at me, splashing more my way. Now she's dipped her whole big head underwater, soaking her long blonde hair, which she flings back quickly, making her hair roll over her head and fall into one tight log around her face. She arranges this log into a giant, wet curl that falls around her forehead and ears like a wig. It drips wetly over her blue eyes, her ear-to-ear smile, and then down her shoulders, into the lake.

"I've got George Washington hair!" she shouts. We laugh so hard at this, she does it again. "Now I'm Martha!"

We've been studying President Washington in history class, and did well enough on the test that Daddy brought us to the lake today as a reward. He sits waiting for us in the car. He folded the seat all the way back as soon as we got out, and is probably snoring away.

Cathedral Rock glows in the late afternoon sun from across the bay, looming larger than any cathedral, its domed shape showing off the flat side that faces us. Reddish at its peak, layers of sandstone change color down along the face, finally turning from red to orange to chalky gray near the water's edge. Desert varnish—dark rust in sandstone that forms over eons—streaks the face of it, its brownish red paint-spill colors running to the water, visible even from across the wide bay where we swim.

The deep blue of the lake in front of Cathedral Rock reflects the even bluer sky and carries a low humming sound, a sound you can only hear if your ears are underwater, tuning in to far-away boat engines. The engines of distant tiny airplanes drone on from somewhere far away, floating lightly through the sky like dragonflies. The sounds of planes and boats tell a tale of people exploring scenic canyons within canyons from the air or water; camping on beaches that only boats can reach, and only planes can see. The body of the lake is vast, stretching long and wide with arms and fingers of hidden canyons everywhere for hundreds of miles, inviting adventurers into secret blue bays alongside windswept rosy cliffs. Today, Cecily and I swim at the public beach, close to the boat marina and a couple of miles from town.

The beach location changes all year because the lake is rising quickly; much of the Colorado River is blocked from flowing downstream by the now finished Glen Canyon Dam. The government made a new beach and parking lot this spring, but will have to move it higher again by summer's end, because the rising lake is already swallowing it up. When we first moved here, we had to walk far after Daddy parked in the sandy lot. But I'm in sixth grade now, and the water has risen so much that the walk from the car to the beach is short; even Mama brings us out sometimes.

People who study the old cliff ruins found here say the government is wrong to turn this river into a lake; many Native People here say so, too. The Hopi say it's burying their ancestor's pueblos built throughout Glen Canyon. These ruins are drowning under rising water, the ancient voices of those who lived there muffled forever. Many of those flooded sites were sacred, too, with petroglyphs that told stories about what their ancestors did there. Some sites had map carvings giving directions between special places; others had sun maps showing times for planting corn. Many Native People still lived in this canyon country or grazed their sheep here. They can't gather herbs there anymore, or grow crops in the rich river loam. They had to leave before the rising water flooded them out.

Many nature lovers and river guides who love the beauty of this canyon country also say it's wrong to build a dam. They wrote books about the loss of a flowing river where native birds and fish lived. Where annual floods nourished the soil. They say the desert wasn't meant to be green, and that making electricity for growing desert cities isn't a good idea, either. Sometimes people carry signs protesting all these things in front of the visitor center above the dam.

My friends and I see the signs the protesters carry and books people write, we hear these distant stories and fights, but they happen high up, far over our heads. We don't really know why so many people are still mad, and nobody asks us anything. Our parents don't seem to care about the stories, their eyes and ears are closed tight. They work for the government that dammed the river. My friends and I stay out of trouble with everybody.

And we get to swim in a lake so beautiful, we don't have words for the living dream that is this scorching hot sun, bright blue sky, and red rock cliffs that drop into blue, blue water. It's all we know, so breathtaking and so harsh, and we're living right in the middle of it, inside the story of it—the dam builders, the river guides, the Mormons, the drowning ruins, and the Native People and the lake. We talk about it and we don't. It's just everywhere.

Cecily and I float on our backs now, closing our

eyes to the heat of the radiating sun, taking deep breaths to keep our bodies afloat. Reaching her hand out, Cecily silently takes mine, as I reach over to lay my foot on hers and make a human raft out of us. We laugh, floating quietly this way for a few breaths, then we drop hands and tread water, racing each other out away from shore. Cecily and I are strong swimmers.

The sinking sun is lighting up the western sky, shading the east side of Tower Butte into a moving tapestry of violet and magenta. The sky brightens behind it, glowing pale orange colors, mixing in with shades of hazy blue. The solemn face of Navajo Mountain brightens, its pale ghostly body catching light, revealing small canyons all along its rocky sides.

Suddenly, we both hear my dad, whistling and waving to us from the shore to come in. We turn and swim toward him, swimming steadily then standing up as our feet touch the sandy bottom. Making our way over to our beach towels, we lay down to dry off for a few moments. Daddy turns and heads back to the car, knowing we'll follow, and we do. Taking turns patting each other dry, we pull shorts on over wet swimsuits and shove thongs gritty with sand onto our feet, muddy water still running down over our toes.

We run to catch up to Daddy, who is making his way back to the car. I turn my sunburned face toward the lake and stop to watch the golden and indigo sky. I smile a goodbye, knowing I'll be back soon.

CHAPTER 26

The Road To Indiana

When the school year ended, we'd travel back to Indiana to visit family. Mama and Daddy were from there, and almost all our relatives still lived there. I'd be cheering the end of school one day, and the next one I'd be packing my clothes, and some games and toys for a very long road trip. I loved being in Indiana, but the achingly slow days it took to get there from our desert were grueling. I felt the slow passage of every mile, or it seemed that way.

I'm eight, or ten, or twelve years old, lying under a blanket on the plastic bubble-covered back seat of Daddy's blue 1968 Buick Electra. The plastic is icy cold and clammy. It sticks to my bare legs. It's the first dark morning of the trip, and a few stars are still awake. I'm awake too, yawning after Mama shut the car door once Sandi and I crawled in. With eyes like slits, I look out the window and down the street over the desert. There's a pale yellow sliver of light along where the sky meets the earth. I fall back asleep as Daddy backs out of the driveway.

When I wake up, we're speeding down an empty road, somewhere in the middle of the Navajo Reservation. Through the window, there's a wide-open desert landscape—the Vermilion Cliffs looking gloomy on one side, vistas to the horizon on the other. The sun is bright but low, shining long shadows between hillocks and mesas, out across an empty valley.

I doze again. When I wake up this time, we're on the winding roads of the Hopi mesas. We're on First Mesa, driving to Second Mesa, then Third. Staring out the window at nothing, the car finally slows as we come to the pueblo of Old Oraibi, on top of Third Mesa. Mama likes to stop here when we come this way. These pueblos are built high on a mesa, like our town. They're flat, though, not built in the cliffside like the old ones. Many families live here—grandparents and cousins, too, all in the same house, attached to all the other houses. Daddy coasts into a gravel lot and parks the car. My sister and I know this is one of the only stops he'll make all day today.

"Kids, you can get out. Girls. Come out now," Mama says, but I want to stay with my blanket. Sandi sits up though, stretching, and then slides over and gets out, so I decide to follow her.

Mama is reading a sign in the parking lot that says this pueblo is very special, it's the oldest village in our country. People lived on this mesa for a long time before our country even had a president. But we're tired of standing there, so Sandi and I leave Mama at the sign and walk over to the brown building that says 'Store' on it. The 'Open' sign shines in the window. I touch the rough, dry wall with my hand as I walk into a cool room. The wall is made of mud and straw. You can see the tan straw, stuck in the dry mud.

Inside, the store has crowded aisles filled with shelves of canned food, fruit, batteries, and, at the bottom, large sacks of Blue Bird flour. The ceiling is low and made of round logs that run the whole length of the room. I find the candy aisle and pick out a Three Musketeers bar and some Junior Mints. Up at the counter, a cheerful woman wrapped in a shawl welcomes us. We say hello, but then see piki bread in a basket. Piki is fun to eat, even though it's like chewing on dark blue-purple sandpaper. It's thin, brittle, and rolled up tight. The Hopi only make it during holy days or for dances, so we don't have it very often.

Mama has come inside now. "It's made from blue corn ground on a large, flat stone called a metate. It's the same kind they find in ruins, from all those years ago. Then they mix some ash from the fire into it, and water." The woman smiles behind the counter, as I roll my eyes at Sandi. She nods her head, silently. Mama tells us this like it's big news, every single time we're here. Like the heritage sign out front we read every time we stop here.

The piki breaks easily, so I unroll its stiff curves slowly, as we stand outside the store. A light wind blows sand around our feet, and long shadows hide the dirt streets of the adobe village. The piki doesn't unroll far before it cracks apart. I pull small blue-ish pieces away, popping them in my mouth. Once I put a chunk in my pocket to save for later, but it crumbled back into sand.

"Mama, where is Indiana? Is it where the president

lives?"

"No, it's not that far, but it's a long way from here," she says. She purses her lips, then looks away. I want to ask her how long it will take to get there, but I look at her frown and decide not to. And it's still morning, so I snuggle into my pillow and blanket when we climb back into the car.

The sun is high overhead when I wake up again. Rubbing my eyes, I sit up and find Sandi staring straight at me, like an owl. "Scoot over!" she hisses, like a snake, ready to bite. I stick my chin out at her, my eyes narrowing into tiny slits. She rolls her eyes again and again back at me. We're quiet in our meanness so Daddy doesn't hear. Drawing a pretend line right down the middle of the plastic-covered back seat, she whispers: "If you touch *even one finger* on my side, I'll slug you. Pow! I'm *not* telling Mama first."

I wrinkle my nose at her and turn away, coughing, letting her know she stinks. I'll stick my finger over anyway, when she's not looking. And then, a minute later, I do—but then, smack! She *was* looking, after all.

"Waaah!! She hit me! Mama! She smacked me! Hard!"

"She was on my side! I told her not to, Mama, but she did it anyway!"

"No, I didn't! You just hit me! Mama, she hit me," I sob.

"Girls, stop it right now! Both of you, move to your own side. And stay there. I don't care who started it. Don't make me tell you again." Mama turns back around, looks at Daddy, shakes her head and sighs, then stares down at the map in her lap.

We travel the whole way across the country like this, hundreds of miles a day with few breaks. Our fights over the invisible line down the middle of the seat, or the etch-a-sketch or slinky, is the universe inside the car, while the actual universe rolls by, unnoticed. We could be awful.

We're little, though, and Daddy hardly ever stops. If we keep fighting after Mama shushes us, Daddy steps in.

"Stop it! *RIGHT NOW.* Do you hear me? Do you want me to pull over? Do you?"

I'm afraid of him. Sandi is, too. And not just in the car. The arguing stops—for a moment— after he yells at us, though. Not because the problem has gone away—needing to stand up and stretch— but because both of us know what might happen if he does stop. It's true Daddy's stuck behind the steering wheel, driving. But he screams at us loudly, his face big and red, the car a low-flying bullet swerving across the road as he does. We have good reason to fear him. But he wants to get to his stopping goal, so we're mostly safe when he's driving. We need a stop, but a stop was also a threat.

At home it's another matter. He'll get so mad so fast, like a pot boiling over on the stove. It happens often and involves belts, swats, or slaps that can leave bruises. Mama never says a thing about it to him, either. Once, when my sister was in second grade, he bruised her legs badly. She wore shorts to school the next day, hoping someone—maybe a teacher— would see the bruises, and ask her what happened. But no one said a thing about it. I cried too when he made my sister cry. I hated Daddy at those times, my heart an iron shield against his cruelty. I hated Mama, too. I thought she would help us. Even after years of not helping, the next time it happened, I thought she would. But she left us to face the sharp spear of his anger, alone.

~

Shorter day trips with him are fun, but long road trips to Indiana aren't. He wants to get there, and fast. But toward the end of the travel day, a miracle happens. He pulls off the highway and follows a road into the streets of a small town. We cruise along the quiet streets. A Best Western motel with a swimming pool suddenly shimmers in the heat ahead, and Daddy at last pulls into a parking lot and stops for the night.

And so, I'd make it through each day, counting the miles between the black dots on the map that were towns, adding up how far it was until we'd stop. Set free ten seconds after we parked our tired, creaking blue Buick at the motel, Mama would reach into a bag by her seat, and hand my sister and me our swimsuits for a quick clothing change in the room. Grabbing bath towels there, we'd race to the water, yelling and running barefoot across hot black pavement. Tossing the towels onto a chair inside the pool gate, we'd fly through the air, birds without wings, legs up in a ball, and land—ka-boom—in the deep end of the pool. I'd swim underwater and come up in the middle of the pool.

"Sandi! Dive off, and swim through my legs!" But

she'd climb the diving board, and do another cannonball instead.

"Woo! Here I come!" Diving deep now, she'd swim underwater to where I was—which changed as I kept backing up to the shallow end—and make it through my legs. Surfacing behind me, she'd dunk me underwater.

"You cheater! You kept moving!"

We'd both learned to dive off a board and swim the length of a pool underwater. I also liked to dive deep, and sit on the bottom of the pool, and then exhale upward, leaving a trail of bubbles behind. We'd practice our swimming tricks at the end of each day, falling asleep afterward with our pajamas half on. The hours spent picking at each other in the car fell away. The pool washed us clean. It changed us back into ourselves, after a day of blurry scenery changing from flat and green to sweeping and hilly.

~

Driving across the country, our fighting sputtered in and out as the scenery changed outside the rolled-up back seat windows, air conditioning pumping away. The vibrations of the car on the road rose up through the tires into the seats and into us, keeping us awake or rocking us to sleep, often at the same time. The slow-motion changes brought us a flat, diminished reality outside the car world— a kaleidoscope of color, Gulf or Texaco gas stations and Stuckey's roadside stores, and towns so small it was miles to the nearest building once we saw the 'Welcome' sign.

Desert, mesas, and pueblos of our first day of

travel gave way to shades of green desert, from brilliant red rock of western New Mexico that looked like our mesa, to scrubby desert eastern New Mexican plains that flowed into prairie as we crossed the border into Texas, then Oklahoma. Prairies were like deserts; you could see to the end of the earth, but they were oceans too, as wind blew tall grasses and wildflowers, moving ripples of waves across the lands. It was easy to imagine tall ships sailing across this grassy ocean, sailing west with strong winds filling their sails.

The flat prairie scenery shifted into green fields with corn sprinkled on top, corn that grew tall on both sides of the road, almost making a tunnel that we drove through, a blur of green, tasseled with gold. Then, at day's end, the car would sputter, slow and stop. There'd be another motel with another pool, its clear, cool water inviting us to swim and play once more.

The world outside the car window melted from scene to scene. Now it's shiny green, with wide-open grassy fields turning into small hills. By afternoon, those small hills have grown into larger ones that the road hugs tightly, as it dips and curves, with the dip hiding a creek running through covered by green, thick trees. Here, we'd often find little towns selling local goods by the roadside, or we might even find a traveling circus with a Ferris wheel, out in a field.

"Can we stop and look?" I'd ask. "For an hour, Mama?" Daddy sat silently behind the wheel, staring, intent on the road ahead.

"No. Your dad has the driving route planned out, and there's no stop here. You know that," she'd say. "We *may* stop on the way home. If there's time.

~

Finally, it was the very last driving day. We were getting close to Indiana when we reached the big rivers. First was the Mississippi, where a tall, golden arch at the edge of a huge city framed the first glimpse of it. A river as wide as an ocean, a river as big as maybe ten Colorado Rivers. Daddy slowed the car on the long bridge over the Mississippi so it seemed to take forever to cross as we watched, faces pressed up against the window, waiting for the edge of the shore to pass underneath.

On the other side, Mama sat up taller like she was waking from some dream. She'd start humming "Yankee Doodle" or "Camptown Races." Soon she'd get to "The Wabash Cannonball," a song about a train. She did this every summer, when we reached the shores of the big rivers. We were close to where she and Daddy were born and went to school, and she must have been excited.

"From the great Atlantic Ocean, to the wide Pacific shore..." She'd hum the train song tune when she didn't know the words. I didn't know this song, and neither did Sandi, so we just listened. We'd look at each other, surprised, then watch her. Mama was happy! I was happy, too. Soon we'd pass by the Wabash River, which wasn't as fun as hearing Mama sing the train song. But the Wabash was the Indiana state line. We'd just left Illinois.

"Girls! There's the sign! *Indiana!* We're almost there!"

And then, finally, right before we got to the Indiana town we'd rode for days to get to, Mama pointed to the last big river.

"Look! Right through the trees! See?" Mama's voice was hushed: "It's the Ohio." The car rolled on.

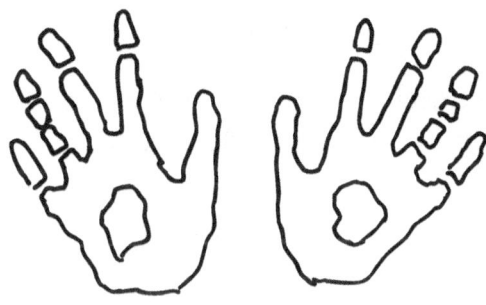

CHAPTER 27

Embraced By Family

"We're here!" Daddy yells an hour later, as the slow-moving car creaks into the long, narrow driveway of a red brick house. He shuts off the car, yawns, and stretches his arms.

"Jesus, what a drive." He opens the car door slowly and stretches his leg outside onto the ground. I want to get out too, but shyness suddenly finds me—I'm not at home, and I haven't been to this house for a year. After all the wanting to be here, the long crawl across the country, the fighting with Sandi, I finally open my door, too. Grandma and Grandpa are standing on the front porch smiling widely, looking down the driveway, their faces bright. Grandma walks slowly toward the car and sees me as I stand up, and her smile widens to cover her whole face.

"Oh my goodness! You've grown so much! Look at you, a head taller! Both of you!"

She stretches one hand out to me and the other to my sister. I take it, looking slowly up at her, at her glasses, her grayish-brown hair pulled back into a bun, her pleated flowered dress. The three of us walk toward the porch, arms around each other.

"Come inside, all of you, and rest a while. What a drive! I've got some iced tea I just made for you all this morning."

I look up at her again. How familiar she is, even the rose-water scent of her, but different, too. She's not as tall. I come up to her nose. I'm so relieved to be out of the back seat of the car. Off the bubble plastic that sticks to me no matter how I sit.

Holding Grandma's hand, I glance around the yard, at the old brick fishpond and the bright flower baskets hanging below the white window shutters on the house. The red brick is pretty, like the color of my cliffs at home. I'm so happy seeing this house I love, a house with secret corners and stairs and rooms. And to be with Grandma. I smile up at her again as my sister and I walk up the porch steps with her, still holding her hands.

"It is *so far*, Grandma. Guess how long it took to get here?"

"Yes, dear, it is! It's terrible. It took you days. I'm so glad you made it." She smiles down at my sister and me again, as we open the screen door into the house.

"We drove out two autumns ago and saw you all. It is far! Your mother and daddy took us to the Grand Canyon. You both came, too. Do you remember that?"

"Oh, I do!" Sandi says.

" Oh, yeah! I forgot! I hate the Grand Canyon, though. It's so hot. There's nothing to do there."

"Well, I recall you caught quite a handsome lizard. You showed him off before you let him go."

A while later, I drag my suitcase up some stairs, following behind my sister's bag: clunk! clink! It bangs each stair, all the way to the top. The door to the staircase is a small wooden one in the hallway. It looks like it might hold shelves of food or brooms and a vacuum cleaner, but instead, it holds the best secret of the house. When I open the door, a steep wooden stairway appears in the dim light. The light brown stairs are narrow and shiny. They lead up to Grandma and Grandpa's attic. The roof slopes down at the eaves, but we climb up with our suitcases and find it's still tall enough for us to stand up in. The ceiling is made of wooden boards too, and there's a big window to sleep under. It looks out over the large, heavily wooded sloping backyard. I love sleeping up here in this secret place, away from everyone downstairs. We unfold the cots we find here and fluff up the sleeping bags and pillows that go on top. After stuffing our suitcases under each cot, we yawn and lay down for just a minute. The soft bed and sunny quietness feel just right.

The next morning, Grandma is waiting for us in the kitchen when my sister and I come downstairs.

"Good morning, girls! Oh, heavens! It's just so good to see you in my kitchen again. But eat your breakfast now, I poured you some fresh orange juice. Your mother and daddy are out on the back porch with Grandpa. Let's say the prayer first."

"I don't know one, Grandma."

"Oh, girls. Well... *Komm, Herr Jesus, sei unser Gast; und segne, was du uns bescheret hast. Amen.*

Do you remember it, now? We say it in German, like when I was young."

Sandi and I smile up at Grandma. "We don't say it at home, but I remember some of it. A little. Grandma, do you speak German?"

Grandma lifts her head and pauses. "I used to, honey. But we don't speak it much anymore. Not since the war. Almost no one in town does." She paused. "Maybe at home, they do." Grandma is quiet at the sink, washing dishes. She stands there, looking out the window. We're eating our warm creamed wheat and orange juice when Daddy comes in from the porch. "Lets go, girls! Get dressed, we're taking off now. Going to see your mama's aunt and uncle."

"Oh, give the girls a minute. They just sat down to eat." Grandma gives Daddy a smile. "My impatient first-born."

Daddy stops to look at Grandma, nods, then looks at us. "Well, okay. When you're done, though, go straight upstairs and get dressed. We don't want to have to wait for you."

Aunt Leona's house is square and white, and it has a whole second floor upstairs with a bedroom. Its covered front porch swing holds my great aunt, who is swinging as we pull up. She stands to meet us as we park, her face lit up as she comes down the steps to the fence gate.

"Oh, my. Look at you all! What a sight you are! It's been so long." Uncle Romey, smiling, comes out of the house now, springing lightly with his cane, to greet us. Sandi and I are out of the car, and they give us a big but quick hug, then turn to Mama, behind us. They join arms around her and hug her hard, with tears in their eyes. "Oh, look at you. You look so good!" They're so happy to see her, and I'm dancing around because of the hugging. I'm not sure why they're hugging Mama so much. She stands still with her arms around both of them, smiling right back, but her eyes seem sad, too. Daddy stands next to her, not hugging anyone, with his hands in his pockets, watching.

"Let's all go inside and sit down so we can visit! Oh, I have been looking forward to this day. I've been marking days off my calendar. I sure have missed you. I have some lemonade and iced tea. I finished making it just before you drove up."

Soon, Sandi and I are bored since no one really talks to us. We wander out to the porch swing and sit there together, kicking our feet to make it move. We sit there, listening to the chatter coming from inside. The swing doesn't go very high, though, and there's nothing else to do, so I try to shove her off it, and she hollers.

"What are you girls doing out there?" Mama is

suddenly at the screen door, whispering loudly to us. "We've come so far. Look how you're behaving. *Stop it right this minute.* Right now!"

"Mama, I'm bored. I want to go back to Grandma's house." Sandi stands away from me but nods, just a little, not wanting to anger Mama.

"We'll go when we're done visiting. Now come inside and sit still and behave. I spent a lot of time in this house. I slept here often for years when Mother was out at night or gone. Aunt Leona and Uncle Romey, and my grandparents too, took me in when no one else did. You will sit in separate chairs in the living room." My sister and I look at each other, then at Mama in surprise. We want to ask her....

"Go sit now! Not another word!" Sandi, still surprised, stumbles over to a chair by the desk, and I sit on a rug by Daddy's chair, feeling him glowering down at me. Aunt Leona, who has trouble hearing, smiles cheerfully at us and then goes back to her story with Mama.

"You don't say!" she says brightly now to Mama. We sit there for hours, in the small, dark living room.

~

"C'mon, girls! We're going to the park. Get your swimsuits on and bring a towel for the pool!" Daddy whistles for us to get in the car, and then goes back to whistling some tune. We run from the kitchen up the attic stairs and gather our things together, relieved to have left Aunt Leona's house, then race downstairs to the car. This time, I'm glad to get in. We've been to the park with the pool. It isn't very far.

"Will our cousins be there? Are they coming?"

"Yes, they are. We'll meet them there. Your Aunt Margie is coming, too."

These cousins are girls. Dina is a little older than both me and Sandi, and Janna is a little younger than me. In the parking lot, we spy two girls waving at us, standing next to a station wagon. A woman who looks a lot like Daddy gets out from the driver's seat and waves to us. We run over and meet them all.

"You girls are so big now! Mother said you were all but grown up. Come give me a big hug!" We run to Aunt Margie, who opens her arms wide. She looks just like I remember her, I think, as she hugs me. The year since I've seen her falls away, and I laugh into her smiling face.

"Oh my, girls! I'm so glad you could meet us this morning. We've been excited to see you."

My cousins are jumping around, ready to swim, and all four of us run to the pool. Dropping off our towels, Dina and Sandi dive in, while Janna and I sit down and slide into the shallow side of the pool. Aunt Margie walks over to our car, where Daddy stands leaning against the door, arms crossed, a grin on his face.

"Come give me a hug, big brother!" We all watch as the two of them walk arm-in-arm over to a picnic table and sit, laughing about something we can't hear. Daddy throws his head back in that way he has, and laughs hard at whatever Aunt Margie is telling him.

The next morning, Mama says, "We're going over for dinner with your Aunt Margie, so she and Daddy can visit again this evening, so you'll see Dina and Janna again. Just be sure and shower this morning." Mama pauses, looking over at me, sprawled sideways across my bed, my head almost touching the floor.

"Okay." I run my fingers across the wooden floorboards.

"And your aunt said she bought you something for dinner that you really love."

"What?" I sit straight up and look over at her. "Is it barbeque, Mama? Is it the barbeque from a bottle?" The Indiana barbeque, just called "barbeque" by everyone, no matter what kind of meat it is, comes in jars and is soaked in a thick, juicy sauce. It's made here. I could eat it until I didn't feel good. My stomach hears this news from Mama and growls happily.

"Yes, that's what she bought you. You'll need to go tell her right away how much you appreciate that."

"Oh, Mama." I don't like it when Mama tells me what to say, as if I would not say that very thing on my own. I'm not a wind-up doll. Mama doesn't even make things at home we like, doesn't like us to ask. But we eat it, we have to, or sit at the table until we do, even if it's slimy canned peas.

When we get there later that evening, I run to Aunt Margie and hug her anyway, in spite of Mama. I don't wait for her to tell me again. I hope she isn't looking.

"Thank you for the barbeque, Aunt Margie!"

"Oh, honey, you're welcome. You don't have to thank me for that. It's not much. You need to take a few jars home with you. You're not going to be able to eat enough no matter how long you stay." She laughs at me, and I laugh too because it's true.

~

"We're going over to my brother's house for dinner," Mama says absently, at breakfast the following morning. "Get dressed in the next couple of hours so you'll both be ready for Uncle Dave's. We'll go sometime after lunch, so we can spend most of the afternoon there, and visit. Wear your good shorts or the new sundress," she says, looking right at me. "But not those raggedy old, purple things you always have on.

Sandi, wear the blue sundress." Surprised, Sandi and I look at each other. Mama seldom tells us what to wear, or notices our clothing, either. I didn't know she'd ever noticed my purple and yellow shorts, my favorite ones. I decide on the new shorts, so I can run around and do somersaults if the evening gets boring. Mama doesn't have a sister, just Uncle Dave.

Soon we pull into my uncle's driveway and hear the voices of my two teenage boy cousins, and my Aunt Joanne and Uncle Dave shouting and laughing in the backyard. I get out of the car but then stop. Standing on the sidewalk for a few seconds, I look at the house. Yes, I remember it. But it's been so long. I don't remember the inside, though. I drag my feet, following Mama, Daddy, and Sandi up to the front door, feeling uncertain. Suddenly I want to go back to Grandma's house. My boy cousins are older than me. Sandi is just a year younger than one of them. There's no one close to my age to play with. I walk in anyway, after Sandi. We follow the food smells through the house to the kitchen, floating along on whiffs of sweet cake and more, coming from the oven. Freshly shucked corn sits piled up on the counter, next to a pot of simmering water, reminding me I'm hungry. At least I'll have a good meal here. Out back, we find them waiting for us, setting up dinner on a large picnic table, and we're almost ready to eat.

"Hey! You made it," yells Uncle Dave, raising his head above a smoking grill. "My big sis! I've got some burgers and chicken about ready to flip here. Come give me a hug!" Mama smiles and laughs a strange, small laugh as Uncle Dave wipes his hands on his apron front, then wraps his big bear arms around her. Over his shoulder, I see her mouth go straight and quivery. And silent.

Mama would often split Sandi and me up, and so we'd stay in different homes with different relatives. This might happen right after we arrived off the road. We were shy girls and didn't know what was expected of us in each house. With all the newness and shifting beds, it was easier to figure out together. We fought in the car because we were bored, but it was strange here at first, and we united against the strangeness of it, until we were separated. I'd startle awake most nights, and for moments, not know where I was. Our relatives could be loud and funny, but those first days, some were almost strangers, too. Different houses, with unknown bedrooms and unexplored kitchens. We didn't know if we could get snacks from the refrigerator, or if we should ask first, or stay away from the snacks, like at home. Mama was careful to dole out our food there.

Sometimes we played in tiny backyards with white picket fences and tidy vegetable and flower gardens like at Aunt Leona's, whose little gate let out onto a narrow alley where cars were parked in garages behind the houses. Or, we might be in yards so big you could run down a hill, and then another, and still be in the same yard. That was Grandma F's yard, and Cousin Dina's yard was big, too.

We had no relatives in our hometown and few visitors to our silent house, so the flood of people around us in Indiana was exciting, but took getting used to. Being around a moving carnival of families and people got easier. By the time Daddy started talking about packing up for home, I didn't want to leave. I was happy in my bigger family and comfortable in their homes.

CHAPTER 28

The Grandmothers

I loved Grandma F's house. It was peaceful, out in the deep green countryside at the edge of the small city. Here, the houses were far apart, with sweeping areas of grass and trees in between them. Persimmon, oak, and hickory trees grew all around Grandma and Grandpa's land, and horses grazed here and there, among a scattering of red barns.

Daddy smiled a lot. He was back with his mom and dad in the house he grew up in, next to where his grandparents' family farm had once stood. Daddy had a story about how Grandma's parents, Christine and Joseph Caldemeyer—who only spoke German—had owned a farm there. They gave Grandma a corner of the land when she married Grandpa, a piece too steep to grow anything on. Grandpa helped build the little red brick house there, and Daddy was born there. The Caldemeyers were doing well enough and bought more land—a hundred acres of rich farmland down on the Ohio River. Grandma still had part of that land. It had been in the family close to a hundred years, he said.

It was wonderful to imagine the large Caldemeyer farm that had stood next door, where tidy brick houses on small, carved-up lots now stood. But a whole century ago was another time, almost another country. Grandma had a black and white photo of her and Grandpa leaning against an old, shiny black car on the farm. The car had tall, thin white tires, and its carriage top had large, squarish windows. Daddy was a little boy squirming in Grandma's arms, and Grandpa, dressed in a suit, held his hand out toward him when the picture was taken. Grandma's brown hair fell to her shoulders, and she had a pretty dress on. A very tall house with a steep roof stood behind them. The photo sat almost hidden, above Grandma's desk in a little alcove.

~

The secret attic room upstairs behind the wooden hallway door stood waiting for us to open it. It was a hideout during the day, but the house had other quiet places, like Grandma's desk in the small arched alcove off the living room. The alcove had an arched door, too, like a fairy door. It opened outside, onto a small half-moon porch. Grandma's red brick house, the color of desert cliffs, had a steep roof that sloped sharply into different angles. The half-moon brick porch outside the door curved around into the brick walls where small, white arched windows looked down onto it. The windows had white arched shutters, with an 'F' painted in script on each one. Grandpa had painted them there. Grandpa was always busy out working on something in the garage shop, or fixing things around the property.

Daddy used to run away from home to get away

from Grandpa, over to the Caldemeyer farm. Sandi and I heard him talking about it with Aunt Margie one night. Grandpa had a bad temper back then and could get mad really fast. He and Daddy would get into fights, and Daddy would run to his grandparents' farm. He stayed for days or even weeks. Sandi and I never told anybody what we heard.

Outside the attic window upstairs were thick green trees, a whole woods where Grandma's lawn sloped all the way down to a road by a railroad track. I hadn't seen trains or tracks close enough to look at them, but I heard them at Grandma's. Sometimes one would rumble me awake at night, jarring me wide-eyed from a deep sleep, up in the cozy attic room. I'd look out the window and see railroad cars, flashing by darkly in the muddy distance.

At evening time, Grandma would fix dinner, only she called it "supper."

"Yes, it's the same thing you eat at home, the last meal of the day. But we've always called it 'supper' here," she said when I asked if it was the same as dinner.

After supper, we'd head into Grandma's backyard once the air had cooled, into the bursting fields of greenery, where nightfall revealed the great mystery of lightning bugs. Running through the night with my glass jar, trailing the flowing fairy bugs overhead, I'd catch them one by one, adding in scraps of grass and twigs for them to cling to. Setting it down, Grandma's pickle jar became a lantern, pulsing off and on magically to some larger, unknown rhythm. With full darkness came bedtime, and freedom for my twinkling jar. I'd twist the lid off and set them free to fly into the night sky, different kinds of living stars flickering above my head.

The next morning, as Grandma was fixing breakfast, I asked her another word question.

"Grandma, a book from our school library called the little fairy bugs that light up 'fireflies.' Are they the same as the lightning bugs we caught last night?"

"Well, I don't really know, dear, but that is a very good question. I can tell you're a good reader. But we've always called them lightning bugs here."

"I've never even seen one except here! We don't have them in our town." I liked words and wanted to know why some things had different names where we lived. I also loved hearing German words spoken too— here and there by relatives—a kind of code I didn't know and couldn't break.

The floors in Grandma's house were all made of wood, laid down in thin, long strips. The living room had wide chairs with soft cushions, and a velvety couch that you could sink into. Next to the couch were wooden tables with claw feet shaped like a lion's leg. The weight of family pictures on top seemed to hold the table down. The pictures were full of strong-looking men and women— the women with their hair piled high on top of their heads—with stern expressions, dressed in their best Sunday clothing. I hadn't met any of them.

Through the kitchen and down the basement stairs was another hidden place, this one spooky: a fruit cellar and tornado hideout. A small door in the far basement wall opened to black space. The small, dark fruit cellar was deeper than the basement. Three steps led down into its cramped blackness. It was damp in there, too, like breathing in a cave. A bulb on a pull chain hung from the ceiling and, when lit, shone palely into the murky corners. The fruit cellar had wooden shelves that leaned stiffly against the cold walls. Here, Grandma's jars of jam, green beans, sauerkraut, and pickles stayed cool. But she also had large bottles of water stored there.

"Just in case we need it," she said. "We have to be ready, because tornados come through every once in a while. We come way down here if that happens."

Extra space in a house above or below a living room seemed strange, and these secret corners intrigued me. No one I knew at home had a basement, an attic, or wooden floors. No one ever worried about tornados or had a fruit cellar. There weren't fruit trees, at least not big ones, and nothing like Grandma's old persimmon tree that hung wide, shady branches across the grassy side yard. Most houses in our town were box shaped. But houses here had many shapes, and often also an attic and basement. Many had two or even three floors. The upstairs held more bedrooms, and above that, an attic. In Grandma's house, this high secret place, filled with boxes that held old things, sometimes murmured their stories into the night.

~

Mama would take me overnight with her, over to her mama's apartment, which had been the upstairs of a house. Grandma J's place had an emptiness about it. Sometimes it felt like I was there because I'd done something wrong. I liked Grandma J or, wanted to like her, because she was my Grandma too— but I didn't know her well, and, like Mama, she had little to say to me. There wasn't leftover dinner in her refrigerator, or bread and peanut butter in her pantry for snacks. Her brown couch in the living room was scratchy, and a rocking chair made the floor creak badly when you rocked in it. Grandma J was a large woman, and never sat in that chair.

Her place was up high, though, and had a view from what had once been an attic. The house it was in was large and white, with three stories. A set of outside stairs in a side yard took you up and up, to finally reach her front door. Carrying my overnight bags, I'd race up the staircase and turn to wait for Mama on the landing, before climbing up to the door. Once there, I could see into the alleys and the neighbor's yards. Mama took her time coming up with Grandma J, who was always out of breath when she finally reached the door.

It was hot inside, with only a fan whirring back and forth to move the air. The bathroom ceiling was low, and slanted lower over a small bathtub. The ceiling was too low for a shower, but a hand-held water wand was attached to the bathtub faucet. Sitting down in the bath, I'd squirt myself with the wand. The apartment was baking hot by bedtime, so I'd spray myself in the tub before crawling into bed on the floor, my soaking wet hair keeping me cool for a while. The tall fan whirred at high speed, moving hot air from one room to another all night long.

I had trouble sleeping there. It wasn't all because of the heat. I liked seeing my Grandma J, but she could look right at me and walk by. She was loud and big, with red hair and swollen legs she propped up onto a stool in the evenings. I didn't see her much except during summer visits, but she didn't notice if I'd grown or changed in some way. Even if I was standing next to her, she still might turn to Mama and ask loudly, "What grade is she in now?" She didn't tell stories like my other Grandma or aunts and uncles did. Didn't she have some to share? I loved those stories, hearing about the big horse that balked when pulling the buggy, or growing food on the old Caldemeyer farm, chickens everywhere, about things that people did back then. One of the best things about visiting was hearing what people laughed about together. These were my stories, too. I missed the desert, missed my friends, but people laughed here; everything was so green. And Grandma F and Aunt Margie were always glad to see me.

The weeks there were vivid, rich, and deep, filled with late-night snacks, and falling asleep while people talked and laughed, weaving a warm, safe net around me. In memory, the much longer school year dwindles beneath the warmth of those Indiana summer weeks, like wrapping paper around a living gift, which is what those summers were.

CHAPTER 29

At Thirteen: Pretending

It's summer vacation again, starting this week. A soft breeze, a barely warm wind, brushes across my face and hair, carrying the wetness and wildness of deep summer woods and winding creeks. With both windows rolled part way down, I lean back against the car seat as the breath of trees moves over me. I'm alone in the back seat, so I stretch my legs out, taking up most of the space in Daddy's new orange 1971 Mazda. The rest of the space I share with a small antique wicker chair my great Aunt Leona gave me. Outside the window, the twisting, turning roadway flows by as we pass through each town and village. We're driving through Arkansas on our way home, and we'll stop soon in a town with a hot spring and old Victorian houses. We're going to a craft village there too, a place full of buildings that look old, where everything in the store is hand-made like in pioneer days. I bet they sell wicker chairs there.

"You know," great Aunt Leona had said after I'd been poking around in her attic one afternoon, "if you want it, and it's okay with your parents, you can have that old wicker chair up there. If you can fit it in the car with you." We walked back up the stairs together, and she pointed to an old brown chair with woven wicker arms and legs. The wooden seat was missing a cushion.

"I want it! Oh, thank you, Aunt Leona!"

"You're welcome, dear! I'm happy it'll have a new home! It's very old, probably close to a century. It belonged to your great-grandfather. Your Mama's grandfather."

~

I follow Mama past wooden storefronts with wooden sidewalks, water barrels, and hitching posts for horses, into a store that makes candles. A man dressed in pants with suspenders and a hat is talking to a circle of people as he dips candlewicks into vats of melted wax. We stop and listen. He takes each wick tied to a long stick, and dips it into a vat for a few moments, then pulls it up and moves it to another one. He makes big and small candles this way, all the colors of the rainbow in them. I've never been to a store that only made one thing and did it while you watched. How happy he seems, doing this.

I make candles at home sometimes, too, only I use molds of different shapes. As I walk around this store, I imagine living here, knowing how to make all types of candles, not just ones from molds. I'd be making candles all day where people are happy, working together. I'd walk around in my gingham dress with a white apron jumper over it, wearing a white bonnet, too. My apron would have a lot of pockets for all my candle tools and wicks. I smile, thinking about it.

But it's a happy day, walking with Mama, and

Daddy too. I'm pretending as we walk that I'm the only child in our family. The three of us are a small family on vacation, which is almost true. Nobody knows that home isn't an easy place, that I'm often scared, and I don't want to go back. Even though I do. But today, I'm the only one here. Sandi got her first job at the Dairy Queen, and wants to work all summer to make money, so she didn't come to Indiana. I miss her, but I'm glad she's not here. The back seat is roomy, even with the small chair in it, and it's quiet without her.

Now we're in a store that makes soap! I didn't know you could make soap. But there's all kinds; soap that smells like lavender or sandalwood or rose. I still have some money, so I buy a bar of sandalwood, and one of rose, shaped like a rose flower. Maybe that's for Tina. Or maybe I'll keep it.

The next store has a man who carves everything from wood. The aisles are filled with vases, animals, and painted trains of all sizes. There are small chairs and tables, too. The man sits in a corner with tools spread out on a table around him while he chisels a tall statue of a bear. Wood chips fall on the floor around him. This whole store smells so good. I move in closer and watch him carving away; he stops to show me the kinds of wood he uses and lets me sniff and touch each one.

"This one's cherry. Here, smell it," and I do, and it smells deep and sweet, like nothing I've smelled before.

"This one's oak, this darker one here is maple." I smell them both. They smell ripe, or earthy somehow.

"Is it hard to carve?"

"Not anymore! I've done it since I was your age. But some woods are softer or just easier to work with, that's for sure."

"Do you make wicker things? My aunt gave me an old wicker chair. It's pretty, but a little dirty. It's not like anything here."

"No, wicker is a different kind of work. It's probably made of reeds or willow, if it's really old."

"She said it was. It used to be my great grandfathers— Mama's grandpa."

"Well, that is indeed a special thing to have!"

All the woods feel different, too; some are soft or grainy and hard under my fingers. I don't think we have trees like this in our desert, but we have juniper. And pinyon, too. They smell really good. Sometimes we go pick piñon nuts.

I leave him and walk through aisles filled with wooden puzzles and toys. I choose a wooden hand-crank puzzle. Turning the handle makes two pieces of wood swivel and slide back in forth in their grooves, while the handle does a circle dance, over and over. Taking it up to the counter, I count out the exact amount, so I only have a couple of dollars left now. I have some pennies, though, and stop at the bubblegum machine by the door and plunk them in. Three huge, fruity gumballs slide out, and I pop them all in my mouth together, their sweet soft taste filling my cheeks up.

"We need to get going," Daddy says to Mama and me. "It's still an hour's drive to our motel."

Daddy doesn't seem to mind stopping so much on this trip back home. Alone in the back seat, with Mama and Daddy in the front seats, I run my fingers over my treasures as we're heading toward the desert. We have lots of miles to go; we still have tomorrow and the day after, so my chair and I get the whole back seat a while longer. I've never been alone on a trip with Mama and Daddy. Not even once, unless it was to the doctor. It's so quiet, so good, I want it to last and never stop. Maybe one day I would miss Sandi. Or maybe I wouldn't. Well, I do miss her a little, but just barely.

"Mama? What's a mason? A Freemason? Aunt Leona said great grandpa was one. That he used to sit in that chair at a lodge. A Freemason place."

"Oh, I didn't hear her say that! Yes." Mama was quiet before she spoke again. "Grandpa was a Freemason. He was a thirty-third degree Freemason, in fact. It meant a lot to him. He was the landlord of the lodge, I think, or something like that. He had keys and used to keep it clean. I'd walk down and see him sometimes when I was a kid. He'd always be sitting in that chair at the door, talking to people." Mama seemed to be thinking, but said nothing.

"Mama? What does thirty-third degree mean? What do masons do?"

"I don't know, really. Community things, I guess. I do know that it took him a really long time to get to the thirty-third degree. He was proud of that, and proud that he went through the ceremonies in German first, and then he did the whole thing again in English. Took a lot of years. But the ceremonies were secret, too. I don't remember much."

"Mama?"

"What is it now?"

"I just wondered why you went by yourself to see him." Mama was quiet again, and for a long time.

"I don't remember. I guess I didn't have anything else to do."

I don't understand much of what Mama said, so I decide to just sit back. I look over at the chair, wondering about it. So this grandpa was in a secret club of some kind. I couldn't wait to tell Tina.

~

The next morning, we stop in another craft village, also built to look like a pioneer town. This one is painted red, though, like the barns near Grandma F's brick house. Mama walks into a store that makes pottery, and I follow her, looking around the shelves. Right away, I find a buttery brown coffee cup, speckled with colors. Writing on the front says 'Booger Hollow' in big letters. I laugh out loud and take it over to show Mama.

"Booger Hollow! Oh, heavens, no! Don't you dare buy that awful thing." Right away I love this cup named after picking your nose, and I want it to show my friends. I rush up to the counter after Mama leaves the store, and with the last money I have now—eight quarters—it's mine. I skip out of the store over to the car, and get into the back seat.

~

I had that cup a long time. I never dropped it or lost it as a child, but then I somehow did both as an adult. I had it for a lot of years, though. Its contents mirrored the times of my life—first, it held seeds and fossils, then embroidery thread; later, spare quarters and dimes hid a marijuana joint. The wooden crank puzzle is still here on a shelf, though, and still moves and dances when the handle is turned. After fifty years, I keep it, remembering that Indiana trip, where I had the whole back seat, and Mama's scant attention. And remembering too, Mama's baleful look when she discovered I'd bought the Booger Hollow cup after all. I still have the old wicker chair, too. It's close to a hundred fifty years old now, a chair that a great grandfather I never knew sat in when the child my mother once was stopped in to visit him on lonely weekends.

I was happy on that trip. Maybe the freedom of that road trip gave Mama something that was missing. Maybe having one child was okay, was manageable. Whatever it was, the mood caught on for the remainder of the trip. There was nothing else I wanted. The gifts I brought home, this time, were mine.

CHAPTER 30

A Confession

The day started out like any other school day. The last bell rang, so I grabbed my sweater and lunch bag and waited for Tina, like always. We walked home together, taking back-alley shortcuts, until we reached the turn-off spot on Elm Street. There, she went up one way, and I turned down toward Gum Street.

School was boring. It dragged on and on as we lurched toward the school year's end. A few weeks earlier, on a day when not one single thing happened, Tina exploded into song on the walk home. We listened to KOMA Oklahoma City, the only station we could get at night, when they turned the power up. They played all the newest hits.

Now Tina was singing "Close to You" by The Carpenters, screeching it out as "closssse toooo yoo-uuu." I didn't know the words, so I howled along: "aahh-roo!" Tina was hitting high notes so loudly that probably even Mama could hear her. I howled along as we passed Mrs. Johnson, who happened to be out front watering her roses. She looked up, scowling, so we sang and howled louder.

It felt great to be a seventh grader! Especially since we were right at the tail end of the year. We reached the turn-off spot, waved goodbye, and went our own ways. After summer, we'd be eighth graders, the bosses of junior high. But right now, school wasn't over and summer wasn't here. Even with Tina's singing on the way home, life was as dull as it ever got. I'd been telling her that I wished something big, something different would happen. Something that would shake things up.

"You keep saying that. Like what?" Tina asked.

"I don't know. Maybe we'll suddenly move. Maybe I'll find hidden treasure out at the Cliffs."

"Well, good luck with *that*," she'd said last time.

I turned the corner and glanced down the street as our house came into view. Daddy's car was parked in the driveway. That was strange. It was too soon for him to be home, I thought. *I wonder why he's there.* Worried, I ran past the last few houses, slowing down as I reached ours. Turning the front door knob, I walked softly into the living room, closing it with a quiet click behind me. I listened, but no one called my name. Sounds came from over in the kitchen. It was Mama's muffled voice. And then Daddy's. Daddy was crying. Daddy was crying? I came around behind the kitchen, through the laundry room, and peered around the corner.

Daddy stood sobbing, gasping air between sobs, his arm wishboned over his head as he leaned against the kitchen cabinets.

"My Mama! My poor Mama!"

Frightened, I froze against the wall and watched. I'd never seen Daddy cry, never even seen him sniffle at a sad movie, like *Romeo and Juliet*. His sobs filled the air now, as I backed away and scurried down the hall for the safety of my bedroom. Throwing myself onto my bed, I lay there, stunned at what I'd seen and heard, not sure what to make of it all. 'My poor Mama,' he'd said. What did it mean? Was Grandma sick? Did she fall down the basement stairs? Daddy often scared me, but he scared me now in a different way. Confused and tired, I laid my head down, and then somehow fell asleep.

A door slammed—my bedroom door—waking me up. Mama sat silently in my rocking chair, her hands in her lap, the chair still, watching me. Her face was solemn and dark, as it often was.

"Your Grandma F died today. We just found out a couple of hours ago. Your Aunt Margie called." Her voice seemed stern, almost angry, without a drop of sadness.

I sat up and looked back at Mama, rubbing my eyes wide awake, uncertain what to say to this awful news, to her stern face. My brain was scrambled. I loved Grandma, but thinking of her dying was too much—too, *too* much—and seeing Daddy cry made it far worse. Mama's unblinking gaze didn't help. Grandpa had died suddenly two summers ago, so I knew Grandma lived by herself, in her red brick house where we stayed each summer.

But something else was going through my mind. I searched my thoughts frantically, trying to find it—but then—tried to push it away.

It was about the Wish.

The Wish that something new, something big would happen.

That maybe I *made* something happen by wishing so hard.

"She was outside mowing the back lawn by herself when she must have had a heart attack," Mama was saying, an edge of sadness now in her voice.

That was the big, tiered lawn that we ran down as fast as we could. The place where we caught lightning bugs when it was dark enough outside. A place where I was loud and happy.

"What a terrible way to die, alone, mowing grass...." Mama looked at me, but I wasn't listening. I could see her talking, but couldn't really hear her. I couldn't believe what had happened. But the truth of it was sinking in, moment by moment. That Wish. My Grandma. Her house. Tears came to my eyes, but I held them inside. I didn't want Mama to see. I felt her watching me, so I turned my head away. *I don't have any words to say, Mama. My Grandma.* Mama got up from the chair and left, but thoughts flew through my head, all of them bad.

I made her die.

Or at least wishing so hard helped make it happen. Did it work that way? Could I take it back if it did?

I'm sorry I was so bored, I say to the Wish, to my Grandma, to the doubtful air in my bedroom. *I'm sorry I wished so hard for something big. I loved Grandma, but she died, and I probably helped. What a mess.*

Mama came back in, tall and solemn and unreadable. "We're leaving for Indiana tomorrow. I'm calling your teachers now to take you out of school early."

Mama stood in the doorway a moment longer, but I was silent laying on my bed with my face toward the wall. I didn't feel sick, or tired. I didn't feel anything at all. I wanted to be by myself. As if she knew that, Mama for once did the right thing. She turned and left. The air parted around her and then settled back down behind her.

Later that evening, I called Tina to tell her about my Grandma. That I'd be leaving for Indiana in the morning.

"Was she the one you really liked? Didn't I meet her once? But you get to miss the last two weeks of school to go on a trip? No way! How lucky can you get? We're just sitting around in class all day anyway."

I was glad, too, but I didn't remind her about the Wish, which had become gigantic, and taken over my brain. I had to pack clothes to go to Indiana now, anyway, and it was far.

I'm really going to miss Grandma.

Daddy got a trailer hitch for the car that afternoon, so we could pull a trailer back home. He wanted to bring back furniture from Grandma's house. I guess no one was going to live there anymore.

~

With the news of Grandma's death, we got to Indiana sooner and faster than usual, or it seemed that way. But once there, Mama decides my sister and I shouldn't go to Grandma's funeral. "I know about caskets, and I came all this way. It's not fair," I say to Mama. "Why do we have to stay with your aunt instead of going?" I like Great Aunt Leona and Uncle Romey too, with their friendly faces and house full of dark, carved furniture. But I want to go, even if it's okay hanging out at their house. Aunt Leona lets me pick fruit off the trees and go for walks by myself. She lets me swing all I want on her porch swing, and talk to neighbors walking by. But I'm twelve now. Sandi and I have been sitting around for days, while Mama and Daddy rush in and out, bringing boxes to Aunt Leona's porch; they don't have lunch or dinner with us.

"No," Mama says, "you can't come. Funerals are for adults. You wouldn't want to be there at her house, either," she says again, breezing by. "It's dusty and dirty garage and basement work at her house," she says.

I sit and swing, with Sandi, or alone. The boredom returns, even here.

But Daddy says one night, "Why don't you girls come with me tomorrow? You can pick out a few things to keep, to remember your grandmother by."

We go, finally, early the next morning, to Grandma's house. We walk in, and our footsteps seem to echo. She's really not there. I look around the living room, now empty, except for a few wooden chairs. People I don't know are carrying furniture out of the garage. I walk down the hallway, pausing at the door to the attic, but then head into the guest bedroom and find everything still in place. I pick out a pretty lamp and purple doily that she made, and the bedroom's chest of drawers. Sandy picks out the spool bed that she always liked, and a small table. And then we stop and look at each other. We go to look for Daddy.

"Daddy?"

Daddy is talking to the moving people, and turns around sharply. "What now?"

"We picked out some things. I picked out a doily, the chest of drawers, and the lamp with the man and woman on it. Sandi would like the bed and the table next to it. Is that okay?"

"Sounds okay to me. I'll get the movers to put it all in the U-Haul."

That afternoon, Daddy takes my sister and me to an office where he signs our names on some papers for us. A man with gray hair asks us when our birthdays are. He needs to know so he can give us social security numbers like grown-ups have. We tell him our birthdays and sit and wait for Daddy to finish signing the papers. Finally, we head back to Grandma's house, where Daddy left the U-Haul trailer.

At a goodbye dinner that night, my older cousin Dina tells me, "You got those numbers today because you're getting an inheritance from Grandma. When people die, sometimes they leave you things, and money. You'll get it, and then take it to a bank and put it in an account there to save it."

"Did you get numbers, too?"

"Yeah, both Jenna and I did."

"Did your Mama tell you? No one talked to us."

"Yeah, Mama said we all were getting something."

CHAPTER 31

A Surprise and More Questions

The trip home seems fast again, even though Daddy drove slower because of the U-Haul. This time it's as if Grandma's death and watching her whole house emptied hangs over our car, putting everyone in a quiet mood. There isn't much to say. Suddenly we're home, backing the U-Haul into the driveway.

The next morning, my sister and I help unload the couch and tables that were Grandma's. They look strange on our garage floor. They look wrong somehow.

"Do you think wishes can come true?" I ask.

Sandi turns to look at me in the garage and puts down a box. "What? I dunno. Maybe sometimes they do. If you wish hard enough."

"So wishing hard can make something come true?"

Sandi sighs, looking at the box filled with Grandma's things. "I really don't know. Maybe. Probably not." She shrugs, picks her box back up, and disappears into the house.

I carry Grandma's old, painted lamp into my bedroom, looking over the painting on the front. I always loved this lamp. Grandma liked it too, and one afternoon we sat on the bed and looked at it together—at the man and lady on it, dressed in old-fashioned clothes. The man had white hair that curled on the ends, like President George Washington. The woman held an umbrella over her shoulder. Grandma said she liked to imagine what they were saying. She thought the man looked like he wanted to ask the lady something, but that the lady was leaning back like she didn't want to hear whatever it was. Grandma was smart that way, she could look at things, and tell more about them that I couldn't see. She saw beyond what Mama saw. Or if Mama knew things about people, she kept them to herself.

I wanted Grandma's antique chest of drawers to be in my bedroom but for now Daddy leaves it in the garage and covers it up. I decide not to ask him why it has to stay here.

Weeks later, two letters addressed to me and to Sandi come from a social security office. I see them sitting on the dining room table with the other mail. Mama opens both letters that evening and shows me the cards with our names on them. Sandi and I have the same long chain of numbers all the way through, except for the very last one; Sandi has a 3 while I have a 4.

"These are very important cards that you'll need when you're older. I'm keeping them so they won't get lost," Mama says. "It'll be hard to replace."

Later that night, I hear Mama and Daddy talking about Grandma and Grandpa.

Daddy's voice was clear through the bedroom door. "I can't believe they still had money. They could have traveled abroad; they could have done a lot. At least they had the travel trailer, but they could have taken a cruise somewhere."

"I wonder why they didn't?"

"I don't know. They could have gone to Germany to visit relatives. There's a lot of family still there. Maybe there were too many bad memories. My dad's family there lost everything. My mother quit speaking German. Because of the war."

Mama and Daddy didn't say anything more. I was listening, though. I wondered what they meant about the war. There were so many questions.

~

A few weeks later, right after dinner, Mama calls us into the living room and asks us to sit on the couch. I sit on the edge, my back straight as a broom, unsure of what to expect. I wonder if I'm in trouble. *I bet they found out about the Wish.* I clench my hands together, waiting. Mama sits in the chair next to the fireplace, wearing her denim embroidered shirt over a white blouse. Her face gives nothing away.

"I've decided to redo your bedrooms. You'll both get new bedspreads and curtains. And fresh paint, and maybe some carpet. You can look through the catalogs, and probably find something there. But let me know what you find, because it can't be too strange. Nothing tie-dyed."

My sister, wide-eyed, turns to me, says nothing for the ten thousandth time, and my own wide eyes look back into hers. It's good she can't read my mind, because I'm so relieved. It's not about the Wish after all.

To my surprise, Sandi shouts, "Mama! You're kidding! I want to look right now! Today!" Sandi, wide-eyed and happy now, runs for the closet where Mama keeps the catalogs.

One night, in the Montgomery Wards catalog I find it, after long hours of flipping through pages of Sears & Roebuck, and JC Penney. Suddenly, there it is on the next page—a beautiful flowery green and apricot bedspread, with sheer layers of a flounced ruffle edged in lace, that falls softly all around the bed. It has matching curtains and pillow shams. It seems to glow on the page. I take it to show Mama, hoping she'll approve.

"Well, it's a little frilly, isn't it? I suppose it'll do," she says. I can't believe it! And just like that, Mama orders it, and I wait for it to come.

One weekend, there are men at our house, bringing new carpet to put down in the living and dining room, too. The old, tired lime-green living room carpet gets moved into my bedroom, covering the large, cold tile floor. We find mint green paint to match the bedspread photo. Grandma's old chest is cleaned and finally moved in from the garage. Montgomery Wards mails everything to our post office box, and it comes, and it's beautiful. My floor isn't cold anymore, and the bedspread shimmers happily on my bed. There's a new coziness in my room that I love.

I'm so happy, Mama, but I'm mixed up... What happened to the money my cousin said I'd get? Maybe she's wrong? Maybe it got used for the bedroom fix-up? Or did that come from Grandma's gift to Daddy? Is ours gone? You never said a thing about it, Mama, and it mattered because my Grandmother thought of me, and wrote my name down in her will. And because I loved her.

~

Fifty years later, Mama, you finally tell me I can have Grandma F's antique dresser, the one I thought was mine back then, but you kept when I moved out. I still had to ask you for it. You gave it to me because it wouldn't fit in the assisted living place you moved to. We never did talk about the inheritance money.

I looked at the dresser for years in your spare bedroom when I came to visit. I brought it back to my northwest home and refinished it, brightening up its maple drawers—but leaving untouched the secret spot underneath the bottom drawer where I'd carved my initials, fifty years ago. It holds far more than clothing. I look at it and see Grandma and her red brick house in Indiana, and sleeping under the open attic window with my sister. I feel the flush of warm, deep-green nights and lightning bugs. And that childish memory, too—believing I was powerful enough to cause my grandmother's death. Then I hear the sounds of my relatives' laughter, where food overflowed, where there was enough for everyone, even if they wanted a second helping.

Where something lived that I felt but couldn't yet name. Like love, but bigger. Whatever it was, it warmed me. I lived inside it when I was there. I buried it deep inside my skin, and took pieces home with me each summer, back to the desert.

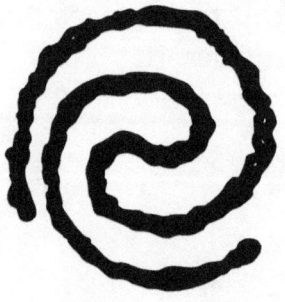

CHAPTER 32

Reflections: The Path To Here

Sitting on my meditation cushion in my house, I breathe slowly in and out. The quiet inside and outside me hold the world. I rest within it. Yawning, I scoot over to my meditation chair, stretch my legs out, and lean back against the wall.

Mama's buried with Daddy now. The house is gone, a lifetime of ninety-four years scattered to the four directions. Mama's death made Daddy's fresh from more than thirty years ago. I thought again about the day he died. I'd been in class at the University of New Mexico when a staff counselor peeked in, caught my eye, and motioned for me to follow her into the hallway.

"Your family's trying to reach you; there's been an emergency."

"An emergency?" Instantly, I froze down to my shoes. "What happened?"

"You can use the phone in my office," she'd said quietly. "Follow me."

My father had died suddenly, sitting in bed watching the evening news. He'd had a heart attack. I was twenty-five then, I remembered, counting back the years. I packed my things that hour, picked up my daughter from school, and the two of us drove through the night to my mother's house. She was there, numb and pale and speechless; her body in another world, surrounded by Donna and a few members of her community church. I was numb, too—in another world, but different from hers. I put our things in the spare bedroom and went into the kitchen to find dinner for my daughter and me.

Lynn's passing floated out of the ether, too, for a visit. She had died when I was forty-nine. From a family of six, today, only Sandi, Donna, and I were left, and Donna seemed gone in a different way. I sat on my chair, weighing all that loss across time in my body, which now felt heavy and tired.

Some universal shift was complete, though, with both parents gone. My sisters and I were next in line. My fears as a five-year-old—that I was doomed to watch my family die before me—had come partially true, although I wasn't that frightened child anymore. I could still feel scared or empty when I remembered those early years, but I felt a lot of different ways at times. I had to make sense of life with very little parental guidance on relationships, social behavior, major life choices, whether clothes matched or not; almost every area I could think of, except, perhaps, reading books. But I had done so.

The richness of my life was satisfying. That richness—hard to describe— took up a lot of space inside me. It was a background, an infinitely quiet sense of *okayness* that never left me, didn't budge even when strong emotions flared or floated through, even if they stayed a while. Sometimes the richness was like a vastness; sometimes it was a great heart warmth. But it was the same peaceful solidness that often radiated out and around me, even in the midst of chaos. Spiritual life had broken open many locked-away places; time and the rock-hard practice of self-love had dissolved many of those newly discovered knots and bumps. Beauty shone through everything. I could look across a sun-dappled yard, the late afternoon light making leaves almost translucent, and be filled, like the leaves, with a profoundly luminous joy that shimmered, that filled and overtook me.

But sometimes loss or pain did, too, and fear for the world around me. The fluid presence of it all together— everything, whether inner or outer— now seemed both ordinary and extraordinary.

I went downstairs and looked at the wall of old family black and white pictures I'd carried with me and hung wherever I lived, as a sort of earthly anchor. Some faces, like my Grandma and Grandpa F's, were warmly comforting and had been my guardian angels for a long time. Some, like my great-grandfather Joseph Caldemeyer, I only knew through stories. The single photo I owned of my mother as a young child with her mother caught my eye. The child, still an infant, looked to be near tears. She sat unsteadily on Grandma J's lap, her arms in her lap, her shoulders hunched forward. No hands reached out to steady her, no arms sheltered her from a backward tumble. Grandma J looked away from her and smiled into the camera. I guessed that photo symbolized a lot of what my mother's childhood had been like.

Yet these faces, hers too, had still moved me forward in life. Their expressions showed that life had been hard. Mine had been, too, and still could be, but maybe that was alright. I thought again about how I'd moved my daughter and me to New Mexico, and entered the great unknown world of college the following year, as a twenty-five-year-old single mother, with no money and no family for hundreds of miles around. We lived on a narrow track for years, my daughter and I; filled with classes, tight budgets, food stamps, music in the streets, scholarships, poor child support, slumber and skate parties, state-subsidized everything. Fear of failing college, with marriage behind me, had built a fire in my belly. There was no back-up plan.

And there was a fierce fight in me, too, to give my daughter a range of choices that I hadn't had. In my family of women, all married young and had children by their late teens or early twenties, including me, a mother at nineteen. I had chosen and planned that, though, and my much-loved daughter remained the center of my busy life. I scheduled my classes around hers. My daughter watched my struggles, and so learned that making her own way wouldn't be easy, but was entirely possible.

After she graduated college, I took her on a trip to Tibet, a destination she chose partially from her interest in world religions, and because I was practicing with a Tibetan master by then. It was made possible though, by an inheritance from the sale of part of the Caldemeyer farmland down on the Ohio. I'd decided the money from that piece of the ancestral lands would finance this once-in-a-lifetime journey and was glad for this unexpected boon that allowed it. My ancestors had been moving something forward all along, I felt; not just for me, but my daughter as well. Their gifts were real.

And I was clear, after the divorce, that I didn't want to live my mother's life, either; one filled mostly with duty toward a demanding husband and four children, with no room for personal choices or college. My life had, in my confusion, begun drifting that way. It wasn't that I simply didn't want that life; I was terrified it was my fate, over which I had little control. I didn't want what larger society said I should—one lifelong stifling relationship, and a house full of children. I wanted to be in the world as myself, and unfold whatever I was to experience, and give whatever I had to offer. The fear faded as years passed, and I graduated from law school. No other children appeared, and my beautiful daughter thrived.

What might Mama have found most deeply within her, had she the opportunity to look, been encouraged to try, or had simply taken a wildly, desperate leap, as I had? The poverty of spirit my mother struggled with was blinding, even after all her children were grown, and money was much freer. No one in my family had been to college. My father, from a lineage of German farmers, implied over the years that it made people mostly useless; it gave them "soft hands." He died before I finished law school. The success of the years that followed were heady, and buoyed me along through many more, until a move to the Pacific Northwest landed me up against an unknown wall of deep longing that was as solid as rock.

But the longing wanted to be known. It led me into an ashram, whose teachings and practices broke open my heart and body, then broke them open again and again. The poverty years of college and the working hours afterward fell away in the face of this newfound vibrance that broke free, that filtered up through all that was and wasn't me. The wall began to dissolve. I began to feel more deeply. Something dark at the core of me was melting, as if it had been frozen for years, or from birth, or from before this lifetime. The visions I often had of vast, peaceful cosmic space flowing through me were a mystery I wouldn't decode for years.

Neither could I explain the deep well of grief that arose in the meditation hall, spilling out through my eyes. I cried deeply and often those first years, laying my head down on the meditation floor and weeping uncontrollably. No memories were attached to this grief. In time it slowed and eventually stopped. It simply felt like heartbreak.

Eventually, though, I left law and policy to find a profession that supported the inner evolution I had passed through. I'd been an intern prosecutor in the local District Attorney's office my last year of law school and enjoyed the challenge of criminal cases and trial work. But I saw legislative law as an opportunity to help elected officials change things for the better for everyone, especially women and children, and not just a particular person in a single outcome lawsuit. I hired on with the state legislature and worked there, researching and writing legislation. I enjoyed the research and the conceptualization and intricacy it took to bring lofty ideas down onto paper, into a legislative format. It could take a year or two, working with the Senate or House chair of a legislative committee to create a significant legislative act that might rewrite the state election code. It was hard, though, to watch the legislative process break down during the sessions and see legislation it'd taken two years to create go down in flames on the Senate or House floor. After enough years, I became disheartened. I also felt distant from everyday people, especially women and children, whose lives I was interested in improving.

A move to Oregon provided a fresh start, and I went to work for a state agency to help start up a new, federally-funded women's health program that would provide free health exams and birth control. This felt closer to my heart, very different from the abstract legislative world I'd known. The move also gave me the opportunity to investigate many schools of spiritual practice and philosophy that had begun to draw me in. After a long search, I was drawn toward a teacher and lineage descended from the Kashmiri region in India. I dove in, and within a year or two, much inner change had occurred.

As years passed, I found myself wanting to work directly with people. Eventually, I found a Jungian-influenced graduate psychology school whose philosophy I loved and whose course was set up for already-working professionals. I joyfully committed to this new direction.

One night after I'd decided to return to school, I had a vivid dream. In it, I was walking through the dark nightfall of a warm, humid jungle. I felt peaceful and safe with the quiet buzzing of night creatures, and followed along a footpath that had appeared under my feet. A light glowing through the trees up ahead caught my eye, and I walked toward it, deeper into the jungle. The glow slowly grew brighter. Soon, I entered a clearing, where the forest-green and gold radiant light intensified. I was alone in the clearing, except for someone sitting silently on what seemed a wooden bench. It was a woman. The light surrounded me, and was mixed with a glowing sort of love that radiated from that same light. It lovingly drew me closer toward the woman. I stepped nearer to her, and saw that I knew her. She was a lawyer—a well-known judge—and someone I admired for her support of women in the legal profession. Cloaked in darkness and beauty, her being glowed with a gentle light. The bright energy of love emanated from her as she raised her eyes to me and held them there, and smiled ever so slightly. I was receiving a blessing. I smiled back in that moment, standing there. I woke up sobbing, knowing she understood my need to find work that was more closely aligned with my heart. It felt like a sort of permission to leave the legal profession.

It was a long process—coming to terms with returning to academia. It had been bone-breaking hard—after all it had taken to get through law school years before—to pursue a new livelihood, but in time I became a psychotherapist, grounded both in Jungian thought, and somatic awareness in the body. One by one, pieces of this great life mystery clunked gently into place, and the rough waters smoothed into peaceful, more often. Spiritual company now was for sharing the always unfolding adventure of deeper evolution, rather than finding some missing part, or a single, awakened life meaning.

The longing, I realized, was just an inside-out version of the peace I had been looking for, hidden in deeply buried and once-painful places. I remembered how my mother and I had both loved *The Wizard of Oz*. I thought of Dorothy, wearing those magical ruby slippers, not knowing all along that she carried the key to the very thing she sought. It felt a bit like that.

Mama's education was through Catholic schools. Daddy's family were German Lutherans, but he'd had no interest in it, as far as I could tell. Nowhere were there Buddhists or yogis; no non-Christian model to follow, no theologians or satisfied faithful to talk to. Mama's cold ways and Daddy's indifference moved me away from the small church exposure that I'd had. I'd taken a leap into an ashram and started my own search for meaning. Life today wasn't problem-free, but I felt equal to whatever was happening with or around me. I could more openly love those around me and let them love me back.

Today I also loved that girl—dark corners and all—who worked so hard, who, early on, faltered in relationships. I had been hungry for love, but afraid of being pinned down. I stopped blaming her for all that not-knowing, and what resulted from it. I came to love her strong, adventurous spirit, and curiosity about the world. I could see from this vantage point of age that every single choice I made, no matter what it was or who it impacted, all got me here, to this solitary moment. I looked again at the family photos. *Yes,* they seemed to say. *It's true. All the hurts and blessings you went through are your treasures. It took every single one of them to stand here today. It always does.*

I remembered how as a five-year-old, I'd learned to walk outside, look around, and find solace. There was wisdom at work there. I looked now across the room to where a large, framed photograph hung. The darkly red Glen Canyon looked back at me as its deep gorge sheltered the ancient Colorado River I'd known as a friend since I was that five-year-old. Nothing felt like home as much as my beloved southwestern desert country I grew up in and birthed my daughter into.

CHAPTER 33

Early Autumn Canyons

On late summer weekends, Daddy would often round us up to go for a drive.

"Girls! Your mother wants to get out of the house, and so do I. Get your shoes on, we're going to leave right now!" he'd yell down the hall.

My sister and I would grab our shoes, tumble out the front door and race for the back seat of the car. We were eager to go anywhere beyond our town. But once we got where we were going, we'd often find ourselves stuck.

"We're driving, we're looking, we're not getting out. That's why it's called a drive," he'd say, smirking into our glum faces.

Mama didn't get out of the car much, either, even if we did. And I'd beg her to when Daddy wouldn't let us, so then I could get out too. I wanted to see whatever was out there. But Mama didn't. Once in the car at a viewpoint stop, I saw her glance at the only other car there, and turn away when the people looked back. We were at the north rim of the Grand Canyon that day. She leaned into her seat, as if to hide from that car. I looked at the people, but they weren't neighbors. I wasn't sure what happened. But I didn't like that she stayed in the car—I wanted all of us to look out over the canyons. On that day, Daddy got out and I followed, and Sandi followed after me. The other car backed up and pulled away, as we looked across a sprawling network of colorful mesas, down to the tiny reddish-brown thread that was the Colorado River.

~

Sometimes Sandi and I would talk Daddy into taking us out to the beach. If Mama came, she'd sit in the hot car, the passenger door swung open, with a leg hanging out. Even in the late afternoon with the sun low, she'd sit that way instead of sitting on a beach towel with Daddy.

"Mama, are you coming?"

"No, I have long pants on."

"Can't you come in pants, Mama?"

"It looks odd. My legs are bad, and I can't wear

shorts."

I looked at her legs after that when she had a dress on, but I couldn't see anything wrong. I knew better than to ask about it.

Whenever Daddy said, "Let's go," I'm ready—but I don't ask him where we're going anymore. He'll just laugh and say, "Why do you need to know?" or "Do you think you get to say where we're going today?" Then I'm sorry—I want to hide from him, my cheeks burning, and not go at all. If he's in a good mood he'll say, "We'll see," if I ask him if we're going to this place or that one. Better to be quiet as a ghost in the back seat.

Now Daddy pulls over and stops at The Cut. South of town, road builders blasted off a giant slice of tall sandstone cliffs, like cutting a piece of cake, and then laid down a road through it. There's a tall, pale pink sand dune spread out against the cliffs right next to the road that we can climb and slide down it if he'll let us.

Daddy parks the car and gets out.

"Let's go, girls! We'll walk down in the wash," he says, moving at a fast pace. "We'll look for agates and fool's gold there." Okay," I say, as my sister and I tie our shoes, put our coats on and run to catch up. I turn around and see Mama, sitting in the front seat, window partly rolled down, watching.

"Mama, can you come?" Mama shakes her head no behind her sunglasses and headscarf. She rolls the car window all the way down, then pulls down the visor, looks into the mirror, and slides lipstick over her lips. I run to catch Daddy and Sandi, then race ahead of them to the wash, excited for the rock hunt. There are agates here, and after it rains, there are pieces of Indian pottery, too, stuck in the deep sand of the wash where the water runs muddy and fast.

"Daddy! Sandi! I found something!" I stand in the wash waiting for them, holding two pieces of agate, found a few feet apart. But, magically, they fit together at a jagged edge, and show a black line flowing around the cloudy beige body.

"Hey, that's neat. I'm going to look here, too." Sandi stops across the wash next to the highway where I found the agates and kneels down to look more closely. I wrap them in a handkerchief and put them gently into my pocket, then look to see if any glints of fool's gold are nearby.

~

If Daddy drives through The Cut without stopping, then he'll follow the steep road down the cliffside, and turn right at the bottom. We'll take that road and follow it, as it doubles back along the valley floor, next to the tall cliffs we just came down. Mama will tell us that this cliff area is called the Vermilion Cliffs, named after a color that's like purple and orange together. We watch them get closer and change colors in the morning sun. The cliffs lead us down to a spot where another cliff ridge joins in, making Glen Canyon, down below the dam. The Colorado River runs through here, at a spot called Lee's Ferry.

We pull into a big picnic area. Daddy parks near a bathroom, by a table with a suncover over it. We get our coolers out and carry them over to the table. Mama says she'll wait for us, and gets back into the car. I give up on Mama, and follow Daddy. We walk to a trail that leads toward a small old mud and brick building, part of an old Mormon pioneer homestead. If you follow the trail the other way, it goes down along the river to a little sandy beach along the Colorado.

The Mormon pioneers that lived here were running a ferry, but also hiding out after causing bad trouble. There's a sign here that talks about the ferry, but Daddy knows even more. People in my town do, too. A hundred years before, a man named Mr. Lee led a group of white men who dressed up like Native People, and attacked a wagon train. The people in the wagon train weren't Mormon pioneers like Mr. Lee, they were just passing through the area on the trail. Surprised, they fought back for days, until the white men tricked them somehow into setting down their guns. Then the Mormon men shot them all, even the women and children. Mr. Lee ran away and came here. He built the mud building to run the ferry and lived near it with two wives and his children.

Daddy says the Mormon Church knew what Mr. Lee did, but gave him money to hide out and build the ferry here. He had a small farm here too, with fruit trees that grew in rich river bottom soil. There's a sign further down the trail by a cabin about the ferry crossing and farm, but it doesn't tell the bigger story, like Daddy does. Whenever I go to the old buildings, I feel uneasy. It's a pretty place, the smells of the river and plants are everywhere, but I don't like staying there long. Maybe the land remembers what really happened here.

Mr. Lee was wicked enough that one day horse soldiers sent by the President came to take him away. They took him back up north to the place where the shootout happened, and shot him in front of a firing squad. Daddy says there's a marker up there about the killing of the innocent men, women and children by Mormon pioneers. That maybe we'll go for a drive up there sometime to see it. I'm not sure I want to, though. I bet the land feels sad there, too.

Today, Daddy turns down on the trail toward the river, and I'm glad. We follow him away from the pioneer buildings. Walking along the trail, the bright scent of tamarisk trees along the river fills our noses beneath dark red cliffs towering above the Colorado. This part of the river, miles south of the dam, flows through high-as-birds-fly, narrow red rock canyons that curve one way and then curve again, looping back on themselves as the river makes its way toward us, toward the mouth of the Grand Canyon.

A hot desert sun warms the canyons, but not enough to warm the water made icy-cold from deeper, colder water being pulled up through the giant turbines in the bottom of the dam, and out the other side into the river. Even miles away down here, the river is shivery-cold. We can't swim in water this cold even though it's a hot day in late summer, but we stick our toes in, wading around at the water's edge at the sandy beach, digging holes and watching them fill with water. We dig a really big hole, and watch it fill up with water that is warmed by the sun. We sit with our feet in the pool we dug.

The Colorado runs fast and deep through the narrow

canyon here. We sit and watch it, too, watch as early afternoon shadows creep across the river toward us, shading our beach. When we get back to the picnic table, Mama gets out of the car and opens the coolers, and we eat bologna and cheese sandwiches and potato chips at the table, enjoying the shade while we watch large birds high in the sky circling near the cliffs. Gliding along, they bank and turn in huge, wheeling circles on still wings, climbing higher and higher toward the sun.

~

A late summer drive might also take us to another favorite place— a purple-hued, wide-open canyonlands area called The Paria. We pile into the car and drive north from town toward Utah to get there, Navajo Mountain becoming smaller and bluer behind us, while gray rock cliffs grow more distant, and the view spreads out ahead of us into a widening valley floor.

Paria is a wild area of cattle, tall clumps of Indian Ricegrass, and deep red mud in a cliff-lined valley. On days when the clay mud is dry enough, we'll turn off the highway onto a rutted dirt road, spraying a cloud of pink dust up behind us. I roll my window all the way down, breathing in the warm smells of early autumn roadside wildflowers, blooming from late summer desert rains. After a few minutes, we pass small open pastures filled with tall green alfalfa grass. No one lives here; I wonder who waters the fields. It's strange to see green fields here in such red dirt, too, but everything seems greener here than in our town.

Finally, we reach the old ghost town of Paria, and Daddy pulls over. We call it that, but the old pioneer town by that name is gone. In its place is a ghost town made up of a few buildings along a single dusty road. It was built by Hollywood movie makers so their cowboys would have buildings and a town. Movies and television shows were filmed in red rock canyons here.

Daddy gets out of the car so we do too, and we walk through the spidery-filled gray movie set buildings.

"You could tie your horse here, if you had one!" Daddy shouts, laughing. The buildings have a long post and a boardwalk out front. We think of movie cowboys, tying horses as they pull their guns out and shoot at each other, and the ones who weren't shot would run away in their tall boots and hide in those still spidery buildings.

The sun is getting low along the cliff top by the time Daddy tells us to get back into the car. We settle in, Sandi and I, tired but happy for once in the shelter of the back seat for the quiet drive back home.

CHAPTER 34

Fairy Flowers, Shooting Stars, Rust-Streaked Canyons: Zion

Our national parks become memory palaces where we spent time with our families.
~ Terry Tempest-Williams

I liked all of those drives, especially if I could get out of the car. But the very best ones were always to Zion. I loved that place so much, that nothing could ruin being there for me, not even driving all the way there for a one-hour picnic, and then driving home.

In Zion, there was more of everything I loved best about the desert. There were more lizards, and more kinds of lizards. There was a river to walk to and wade in, with sandy shores and good rocks to pick through, lined with shady trees full of singing birds. There were trails to wander on next to the river. There were campgrounds nearby to stay in. The cliffs were much closer and taller, and it was warm down by the river on the valley floor, even in winter.

But the last few miles of driving there was the best road we ever took a drive on. Once we got past the park entrance booth where a man would hand Daddy the map, the road entered right into cliffs, into a quickly darkened tunnel, tilting us slowly down to the valley below. This steep road right through the cliffs was the only way down to the valley floor. We'd beg Daddy to honk the horn into the blackness of the tunnel, and sometimes, in the right mood, he would. The tunnel had one traffic lane each way, and had pullouts on the canyon side we were on. We'd stop at the biggest pullout in the tunnel. We'd count them as they passed until we saw it, and Daddy would slow the car and turn in.

Mama, even you would get out of the car here. It was too much to pass up. From the car, we'd catch sight of the huge, open alcove window, already knowing the shock of what we'd find there. The stone window, a large, open arch, was drilled out of the sheer cliff and offered a speechless view to the canyon bottom.

Zion cast a magic spell on all of us. You'd open your car door, Mama, your eyes and whole face smiling at what you could see already—birds flying past the huge open window next to us. We'd dance around you, walking toward it, our eyes filling up with the endless unfolding openness that came into view through the cliff window. At the window's ledge, we'd lean out and look thousands of feet down, clear into the bottom of the heart of Zion Canyon, down where the river ran wildly, but from here, silently beneath us. Far below us, we'd spy the tiny ant-size hole where the road popped back out of the cliff and snaked down the sheer rock face, winding left and right on itself, twisting its way to the valley below us. The cliffs were so tall even here at our lookout window, I had to tilt my head way back and squint my eyes, looking up to see the very top of the edge, and the blue sky above that.

Once we reached the flat safety of the valley floor, we'd stop at the picnic area, parking the car under wide cottonwood trees. Daddy would sometimes lead us across the road to a swinging rope bridge over the river. Sandi and I would stop partway across, jumping up and down to make the bridge sway over the river as it flowed beneath us. Following the trail up to a waterfall, we'd find a thin trickle of water dropping a hundred feet, carving out a small, emerald green wading pool before falling again over a steep ledge, plinking softly onto mossy-covered rocks somewhere down below us. Here we'd sit, Sandi and I, looking out over the tops of green waving leaves of the cottonwoods and the red-earthed valley floor, across to the tall cliffs that framed the canyon.

We'd go to your favorite places too, Mama, where there were hanging gardens. Shade-filled cliffs leaked enough water for maidenhair ferns— slender, little delicate green fronds on black stems—and tiny fairy-golden columbine flowers to grow out of the cracks in hidden red rock alcoves streaked black over red from slowly dripping water. These magical spots were rarely illumined by the late summer sun's fiery radiance. Shooting stars, their fragile pink and purple petals bobbing gently on a single thin stem, grew nearby in the moist dirt piled up over time next to the shady cliffside.

I wanted to stay here. I wanted to live here forever with the golden fairy flowers that grew out of almost nothing. I wanted to find a cave where I could sleep, maybe next to the river, or if we were camping, then there. I was never, ever ready to pack up and go back to our too-quiet home, no matter if it was an hour or we had been camping a few days, because it meant leaving this secret temple oasis behind. Here, quiet meant peaceful. It moved something deep in me, something that told me I was so okay, that I never had to question that again. My small child-size against the grandeur of these cliffs brought reassurance, not overwhelm. I belonged here. The deep quiet and wide canyon spaces here were so different from our house.

One autumn day trip, I surprised Daddy. After lunch under cottonwood trees in the picnic area, he took off walking through deep drifts of dry leaves, recording their crunchy sounds on his new tape recorder. He held the microphone down close to the leaves as he walked, taking care to keep it there. I snuck up behind him, and he didn't notice me following on his heels, matching my steps to his. Leaves crunching from two pairs of shoes grew louder, yet he didn't know why until we were back by you, Mama, at the picnic table, where he turned around to talk to you, and saw me smiling behind him.

In that split moment when I startled him, his eyes widened and his mouth fell open. I didn't know what would happen next—he could be really angry— but he laughed, instead. He laughed hard, throwing his head back in a carefree way; an explosion of laughter erupting after the surprise of finding me on his heels. In that moment, relieved, I laughed too, Daddy and I together—on the same side of the joke. It was a rare thing. I tricked him, and he loved it. The magic of Zion's spell held us strong and tight.

These were the best times, even though we were almost always in the car, with Daddy driving and staring straight ahead, and you, stony in the passenger seat. The backseat required a stillness held for hours without a break or bathroom. Few words were spoken. We sat there, suspended in time, staring silently out the window. For you, Mama, maybe the car cocooned you, as we sped down the road after each adventure, toward home.

~

Today as I write, in the city where I live, it's a rainy autumn day, a beautiful one, the air full of light mist; the trees lit up by brightly-colored leaves, and a quiet sun showing through when clouds part. It's near the date when you died, around the time of year we camped and picnicked in so many canyons when I was a child. I feel your spirit near me, as I have for weeks now, feeling your presence in the full moon last night, and in the dappled light cast by you and the moon through the silent, moss-covered oak trees. They hold a quiet watch for you, an honoring of all the unnamed secrets between us. And today, hard rain comes two years to the day, after you died.

Early autumn now opens a pathway to you. The border between worlds of life here and life no longer here softens and becomes thin. A deep quiet holds; it knows but doesn't speak your name. A stillness spreads out across the land on these evenings, like slow rain that nourishes dry, early autumn landscapes everywhere;

here in my city, in the thirsty deserts, and maybe in me, too. I'm putting my coat on now to walk in the rain, and when I do, you'll be there in the hushed streets, in the droplets and mist, and in the walking.

I miss you, when I can get simple in my feelings, when I get underneath the fractured sandstone layers of memory that were you, me, and our family life together, so often played out in a car, speeding down a desert highway.

CHAPTER 35

Across The Big Rivers

One morning I woke up with a strong desire to go back to Indiana. The notion came on suddenly, the way soul ideas do. There was a solidness to it; it probably hadn't come up before because the timing wasn't right. But with Mama gone a couple of years now, I was startled less and less often, remembering more often she wasn't alive. Disposing of her house and furnishings had trickled to an ending, too. Grieving for her was confounded by the difficult person she had been. It was lonely; full of many kinds of memories I was still coming to terms with—who she was, and who she never had been. And yet, the solidness of who I had become held. I seldom felt alone. There was a bigger love that held it all, even the loneliness, much of the time. My spiritual life held me; all of life was moving on.

I hadn't been back to Indiana for close to twenty years. I'd seen Aunt Margie when she came west one year on a travel tour but hadn't seen my cousins at all. My grandparents and great aunts and uncles were gone except for this aunt—Daddy's sister—who was many years younger than he was. The town was still there, full of memories and places I had loved. I hadn't gone back, though, after delving into the teachings at the ashram and other wisdom schools. Those years were about becoming still, about listening and absorbing the inner changes that the teachings held. And then about leaving law, and focusing on a new profession as well, rather than revisiting special places. But now it was many years later. The wheel of life had spun again, and it felt good to heed such a strong call.

I thought of the cemeteries there, full of generations of ancestors. I had visited them often with Mama, and Aunt Margie, who was the family historian and could tell me about almost all of them, simply as we stood there in the grass looking at headstones. Aunt Margie carried the stories I didn't know, and nobody else did, either. I wondered if she might have stories about Daddy as well. She knew everything about their side of the family. But she knew about my mother's family, too—her mother, aunts and uncles, and her grandparents. Aunt Margie was just like that.

With Mama gone, people might be more open to probing questions about the past. Mama had a hold there. I was still her daughter, and her youngest one. It was her hometown, Daddy's too, but not mine. After visiting as a child, I hadn't kept in touch with cousins, and Mama was somehow in charge of the other adult relationships. They lived far from us; she heard from them regularly and doled out whatever she heard from them like candy at the checkout counter.

But Mama *was gone*. Aunt Margie was still well

and active at ninety; she lived on her own. Soon after the soul wake-up call that morning, I wrote to her about a possible visit. She was enthused, even though we hadn't spoken in a long time. I also called Sandi.

"Hey, what would you think of a trip back to Indiana? Visiting Aunt Margie and our cousins? Maybe poking around town. It'd be fun traveling together."

"Yeah. I've had that in the back of my mind a while too but hadn't gotten around to saying anything. I talked to Dina a while back, though. She told me Aunt Margie was well, but slowing down, at least for her! I guess she's still doing the books for the farmland. Her memory's pretty good, but not like it was. Dina asked then if we wanted to come out, but Mama had just died, and we were planning the memorial service. It's a better time now. Yeah, we should go, and probably soon. She *is* ninety, you know."

I thought about what Sandi said. About how Aunt Margie was well, how good it would be to see her. I thought of Grandma F's house, remembering the attic room where we used to sleep. But mostly I thought of my mother and father, and being in their hometown without them. It felt oddly empty to imagine, as if I had no reason of my own to be there without them. But I had so many reasons I couldn't count them all. And those were just the ones I was aware of.

We decided to do a shorter version of the childhood road trip by driving in from St. Louis. We booked a flight soon after and found ourselves one early autumn day driving out of the city past the Gateway Arch, across the Mississippi River over the bridge that had seemed never-ending when I was a child. And then we crossed the Wabash River, spotted the Ohio south of us through the trees, and then we were there.

CHAPTER 36

The Ohio River

Mama.

It's a late September morning as I stand on an asphalt walking path, looking out over the Ohio River in the town where you and my father were born. All four of my German grandparents were born here too, before you. The temperature is cool and humid now, the low sun promising the warmth to come. The air is still over the wide, quiet waters of the Ohio, reminding me of rivers in the northwest city where I live, but this river holds your history, Mama, and the history of so many others in my family. Carrying more than water, it carries stories of your life. Stories that are mine, too. I'm here to listen for them.

I've come to find you. And maybe missing parts of our family, missing parts of me. To see the old places, and hear whatever your town and our few living relatives might tell me. Your grandparents died before Sandi and I started coming here. It comforts me to stand here, though, to look out at the river, in this place where I have so many young memories.

I've stopped on the path to read a plaque at a World War II memorial along the riverfront. It tells me about the key role your town played during World War II, when the Navy opened a shipbuilding yard here. It produced landing ship tanks, engineered to drive up on land and open a cargo door, letting tanks and soldiers out onto dry land. Aunt Margie tells me that the brilliant design of these ships was instrumental in winning the war; that townspeople—women too— worked in the shipyards when she was little. That my father wasn't one of them, though. An enlisted Navy serviceman, he floated somewhere out in the Atlantic Ocean on a minesweeper ship, meant to disable the threat of German U-boats and help the landing ship tanks built here reach their targets. All of this, long before I was born. And all from Aunt Margie—from here, in this town of German descendants, who were now fighting Germany.

And yet, you were in the Navy, too, Mama. I remind myself of this, knowing so little about it. My father left the country to follow his service orders, but you were here, following yours. The few stories you shared about it were always short, devoid of much that would tell me how you were actually living, and what you thought about life at that time. You worked in Washington DC for a while at the Pentagon—this, again from Aunt Margie—delivering mail, including to the White House.

You married my father one weekend in Boston, when his ship suddenly came into the harbor for a few days, and—somehow—you knew about it. And yet a wedding— choosing someone to spend your life with— must have its stories too about flowers and dresses and hope, none of which broke the surface into words in those later buried years. You and he would go to New York City for ship parties sponsored by the Navy, you told us once or twice. There, you danced to live music by Ella Fitzgerald, Louie Armstrong, or Glenn Miller.

These are facts I know, but they don't connect with much about you or your past. They float like disconnected puzzle pieces in the middle of your life, like my father on that ship in the Atlantic, an island separate from land, not connected to anything else. I'm left with the same, surreal picture of a woman I simply don't know, who could be almost any woman from your town in that period, during World War II. Looking out over the water, I watch swallows dip and turn.

Both my aunt and this historical plaque confirm how little I know about you and my father. What I knew shined a light only faintly on your character, your dreams. The impact of the untold stories was simply carried along in you, showing up in that silent way you moved through a room, through a whole life.

And then there is this town, filled with relatives I knew—grandparents, aunts, uncles, first cousins; many gone now, but so many more that I didn't know. A glance through the phone book is startling—there are pages of people with my father's last name, the name I carry, a rare one in this country. A hundred or more second, third, and fourth cousins show up, all unknown, and I don't know why I don't know any of them. I stare at their names and wonder about their lives.

CHAPTER 37

A Labyrinth

I've been walking the path along the Ohio River every morning this week, smelling the fresh air, watching the birds, amazed at the difference in how the town feels now from those long-ago childhood summers. Arriving here freely by choice on an airplane, rather than as a child silenced for days while traveling cross-country, changes more than a point of view.

At sixty, with my parents no longer alive, I'm seeing everything through the eyes of the next generation. That old child-feeling sets off warning bells, though, telling me I'm an instant away from my raging father pulling his belt off, or from being cut by my mother's cold gaze. I look around but, of course, no one's there. This girl-child is good company though, and sparks fond memories of her adventurous, lightning-bug-loving nature.

I like it here. I like the rolling velvet-green countryside, the historic waterfront area with charmingly restored red brick houses decorated with colorful flower boxes and wrought iron fences. Ancient trees with roots that crack sidewalks open spread their giant leafy branches high; downtown cobblestone streets are sprinkled with new restaurants and shops. The farmer's markets come alive now on the weekends— all so different from what I recall. There are brewpubs now too, a modern trend that this historically German town must have embraced wholeheartedly.

And a German bank called: *The German American Bank.* It delights me. Somehow a sign on an old red-bricked bank building roots me down a bit more solidly. My German ancestors likely conducted business here. Everywhere I look, memories show me I know this place, that my family has wide and deep roots here. And new stories of my parent's lives open this town wider—I have a kind-of belonging here.

Sandi is with me, Mama; we're time travelers sifting through whatever old clues we find about you. They're the next chapter in this life-long mystery board game you left behind. Yesterday we looked for your mother's upstairs apartment where we used to stay during visits. It proved harder than we thought. A cousin—your brother Dave's oldest son— pointed us to the old neighborhood. We parked and walked around slowly for blocks, looking at houses and yards. Time passed; the humidity rose, and the day grew hot.

Walking around a corner, I turned down an alley that felt... vaguely familiar. We walked a short way in and looked around again. A garage stood in the alley behind a house there, and a picket fence encircled the backyard from the garage. There was a gate in it. We looked and waited. The shape of the house seemed right, somehow, set as it was on the property. As we stood looking, I took a couple of pictures and walked a few steps more along the picket fence. From that spot, I noticed an outdoor wooden staircase in the yard, leading up to what looked like an attic apartment.

All at once, memories of the staircase flashed yes, as we both stared. It went up more than two stories, stopping at a landing mid-way where it turned back on itself before heading up toward the roofline. *Mama, look! I'm at the top already. I have my bag, too!* I was again the girl-child who ran up the stairs carrying a change of clothes and pajamas in an overnight bag, waiting on the landing for her mother before rushing to be the first one there.

I stood in the heat. Insects buzzed within our silence. Sobering thoughts came. I now imagined a woman in her seventies and eighties, walking up and down this high, wooden staircase—until that woman moved to an assisted living apartment. Once there, she didn't have to contend with all those steps, although she drank up much of her Social Security pension. That, from Aunt Margie.

Well, girls, it's true that your mother's mother drank. I guess you know that by now. I remember when your Uncle Dave was Chief of Police, and I think he got her in a short line for one of the new senior apartments. The Schnute Apartment complex, it was called. They got her moved in quickly. She had a small pension, but your mother and Dave had to make up the rent difference most months. She never did seem happy there, and it was a new place, too. I dropped her off some extra dishes once and thought it looked nice.

And another story about her, Mama—from that cousin who helped us find the apartment. One day as a small boy in her care, she put him in her old car and sped around the corner, causing his unlocked passenger door to swing open, rolling him out of the car and onto the street. Laughing bitterly as he told this story, he laughed hardest about how—with scratches to prove it— he told his father that night what had happened. Our grandmother lied about it, and said it never did.

You would have hated that story, Mama, hearing that about your mother. It let loose an ancient secret of yours; one of those burning spots of pain you carried, the kind that captivated you for so long. But I was glad to have the story. It pulled a living piece of you out of the darkness, and the sunshine on it made you more real to me, for what you'd been through. I thought about what you'd hidden away all those years. Maybe you weren't so unhappy as a mother, as I had assumed. Maybe it wasn't even very much about your children.

Seeing how life brought your own mother alone to this humble apartment, wasn't something I thought about before walking down this alley. There wasn't enough of a story about it to sink in. You must have been hurt by her choices, Mama, caught in them as a young child, but I never heard you say so. I don't recall you speaking angrily about her, or mentioning events your young eyes must have witnessed. But it's true that your early life was a blank space to me. You must have talked about it with my father, and others like Aunt Margie.

~

Looking at old pictures of you and my father at my aunt's house—early ones before marriage—are surprising, showing a sparkling woman I've never known. Here you are in this black and white photo, sitting on top of my father's shoulders on the front lawn at Grandma F's house. Your face is open and laughing, your body relaxed as you steady yourself, your arms held out. My father is laughing too, bracing his arms together to hold you up. Grandma F's fish pond is behind you, framing your escapades.

And in this picture, you're with women friends circled around a table. Glamorous in your high-necked tailored blouse, you hold a cigarette in your left hand, reminding me you were indeed left-handed, like Grandma J. A drink sits in front of you on the table, while everyone smiles into the camera. A young carefree woman smiling broadly, who couldn't possibly be my mother. But here in your town, seeing your mother's old apartment, thinking about the life you must have had makes this picture of you, maybe with Navy friends, precious—even as it fades in and out of focus.

I think about your parents divorcing when that was probably rare. Your mother remarried and divorced again according to some stories. She bore another child, your much-loved brother Dave, with some unknown man. I wonder if you met that man, Mama. Surely you did, but you never said so. No stories from anyone ever confirmed they were really married.

One day when your Uncle Dave was a teenager, he asked his mother who his father was. He never had been told. She slapped him hard, right across the face! Told him to never, ever ask her that question again. I don't remember who told me that. Maybe it was Dave himself. He talked pretty freely about her at times. Or maybe one of his boys told me. I'm certain it wasn't your mother.

What I'm learning helps me piece more together about you, Mama. Your mother split up you and your much-younger brother, and left each with different family members. You were around thirteen, and Dave was about five when that happened. You lived with your father's family. Your grandfather the Freemason, whose wicker chair I was given; your grandmother who loved opera, and your father's sister, Aunt Leona. Your father didn't speak to his own parents or his sister Leona, so he never visited you at their house.

You loved these grandparents and Aunt Leona, though, Mama, and mentioned how you listened to the Metropolitan Opera every Sunday with your grandmother. You said that lovingly. She took in washing for the wealthier families in the area, who gave her tailored clothing their children had outgrown. She cut down beautiful blouses and even coats to fit you. I spent time with Aunt Leona when I was little, but I never knew your grandparents, or your big connection to your aunt. I never understood what a large hole Leona and your grandparents filled in your life, nor how much you cared for this grandmother, because you had lived with her, apparently, for extended periods. Aunt Margie said that when she died, you were in Washington DC, and the Navy wouldn't grant you leave time for her funeral. She wasn't a parent or legal guardian. You didn't get to say goodbye to this grandmother who stood in as a mother.

For those four years, you and your brother lived apart, because your mother "ran off to Denver with some man," according to Uncle Dave. One story said that man was Dave's father, but no one is sure, because no one knew him. And during those lost years when she was gone, you went to your little brother's new house, and walked him to school every morning. Your grandmother had taught you to sew, and you made him clothes. An orphaned girl-child, mothering an orphaned boy-child.

It's clear now your mother struggled with alcohol, and spent much of what she earned in taverns, where she worked. It seems true that my father's family embraced you, when you had so little structure in your own. I think they took you in, in a way. Apparently, you and Daddy were engaged for years, but waited to marry until the war was ending, to make sure you wouldn't end up widowed with children. But if that's so, I wonder now if you felt you couldn't speak about any of this, having waited so long to marry—that you were lucky to have a future husband, and eventually a family. Many of your friends lost their boyfriends and husbands in that war. Maybe it was better to wall off the past and try to move on after the war.

Finding your mother's tiny apartment reminds me how seldom you spoke about your father. We knew little of him, except that he never paid child support, even when you lived with his parents. Your father— a wealthy businessman—seldom saw you. He remarried, but never had more children. You remained his only child. What part of you simply shut down, when these facts became too thorny for a young girl to bear?

I remember meeting him once; I was eight years old. One summer we drove from Indiana to where he lived in Ohio. We stayed a couple of days in his foursquare, three-story handsome house. My girl-child self walked through room after room, open-mouthed and wide-eyed, marveling at velvet couches, chairs with claw feet, and ornate wooden doors with glass doorknobs—glass doorknobs!—and carved wooden room dividers, so different from our government block house. Although he didn't take us there, he owned an even larger country home outside the city, with acreage and a Christmas tree farm.

Did those decades of silence break open when we visited him that time? Did you talk with him after Sandi and I went to bed? Did you say anything about him to my father? Walking along the steady, blue-green waters of the Ohio River this last morning, feeling the heat of the day rise, I'm recalling that trip, realizing now that you must have wanted him to meet my sister Sandi and me. This father you had nothing to say to, had no stories from. You had nothing in common with him except a shadow of a longing for home, family, place. Belonging.

CHAPTER 38

Arising: Heart Awakenings

In Old Age Wandering On A Trail Of Beauty,
Living Again, May I Walk.
~ Navajo Blessing Way, from The Night Chant

It's our final day here at the apartment Sandi and I rented, not far from the Ohio riverfront. What I'd heard growing up—scraps of ten thousand conversations—mixes with the new stories I've heard here. The mixing is slow and will take time. There's the casual way my aunt mentioned yesterday that my mother spoke with Navy officials after she enlisted, to see if she could get out of the marching-in-formation training because of her severe foot pain. That startles me, but this time I don't ask more. I knew about her disfigured feet, and

264 | DEBBI FLITTNER

as a child I thought they looked strange. In later years I heard her say she seldom got new shoes when she was little. But my aunt's words strike something totally new in me. Snips of images across time fall together. I'm left remembering all the years my mother sat quietly in the car while we went on hikes or explored a dry gulch. And said nothing.

The new facts are settling in between what I knew; it's giving me a bigger lens to look through and see the circle of my mother's life. My own life feels shifted over, too—infused by new stories and new pieces of old stories. My mother's childhood was full of poverty, physical pain and loneliness—so much—and I'm sad for what she silently lived through. I'm stunned that she must have believed that life was simply like this. That even as an adult, she must have thought she had no choice in any of it at all. And maybe that was true.

~

But, Mama, I'm also overcome with sadness for my sisters and myself. And I'm angry at how you kept it all tied up and boxed away inside you, all that pain—bright and sharp, and dark and threatening—pain that swallowed you whole, that colored so much of your life, so ours too. It drew you deeply inward, and captivated you with its consuming fire. It turned you away from us. We became a sort of collateral damage—untended souls caught as silent witnesses to your unsung grief-song.

I had thought that in some ways I was less hurt by your fiery sadness than my sisters, because with three of them between us, I was the youngest and furthest away in age. It scorched me less. But because I was the furthest away, the little love you gave was a faint star by the time any beam reached me. Hardly discernible as anything. We pass down our fortunes and our misfortunes, don't we? We transmit them to the next generation, with eyes wide open and eyes closed tight, through everything we say and do, and everything we don't.

And yet. If I hadn't felt such loneliness—I took some of yours, Mama, resonating like a tuning fork—I wouldn't have searched for what felt like something missing. I may not have wandered outside and fallen in love with the red rock desert, and learned about the tribes that call it home. I'm not sure I would have followed that "there must be more to life" feeling into college, into ancient ruins around the world. I probably would not have been drawn to explore those timeless wisdom lineages, where I found more than I was seeking. But I did all of these things, and because I did, I was at last led into a profession that embraced all of who I was. That grounding allowed me to help others find the same in themselves. I recognize, Mama, that you were at the front of that sweep of time, that you were the spark. I bow deeply, brokenheartedly, to you for all of that.

I'll always feel the echoes of that longing for a mother who could have known the child I was, could have loved her shining spirit. We lived a parallel childhood in this way, Mama. But this week, peeling this pain back one more generation gives me more space to breathe in, it gives me permission to speak about hard times without blame, to acknowledge both your blessings and your shortcomings as the person you were. And it helps me do the same for those around me.

My early childhood also gave me gifts I didn't know were gifts. That loneliness was a springboard from which I launched myself outward, my adventurous self needing to *know*, needing *that* experience. It took ripening years, through all the levels of life, to start making sense of it all. To be brave enough to leave my hard-won career in law, to live instead from the growing softness of the heart.

Weavers in Oaxaca, Indonesia and elsewhere, showed me how women hold the sacred in their hands, and transmit that through their textiles. They craft patterns of symbols to tell their creation stories, and stories of life with their families. They leave a trail of wisdom behind them in their work for their relatives, their villages, for me, to hold and listen to. The Navajo weavers of my childhood did the same. They lived their culture, their sacred origins, over and over through their art that surrounded me for all those growing-up years.

~

All of them taught me that the fabric of life holds and continues on, even when the tapestry threads are terribly frayed. The threads hold, somehow. Some years, Mama, were a journey as far away as I could get from a life that looked anything like yours, overly full of chores and children. You probably had little time for your own self interests. But I also know now that you didn't know how to listen to yourself. You were focused on surviving. You got stuck there.

Yet many years were a journey back to those very things I left behind me, knowing I'd abandoned something of great value. I've claimed my own love of family and hearth differently, Mama. My cabinets overflow with hand-woven tablecloths and napkins in golds and reds and blues; my walls are framed in vivid tapestries brought home from around the world. Vases from far away places hold flowers from my gardens. All of this beauty enriches my daily life, and meals, too, around that old oak table that now sits in my dining room. I didn't guess for ages that what the wisdom teachers were pointing to was the same sacredness, contained deeply within myself. It only required stillness and kindness to discover. I was too young to understand this in the space of those scant years that contained us together in the same house.

Today, at sixty, I understand that much of what transpires in life and in relationships isn't knowable all at once, but remains unnamed, waiting. Wisdom is a truth that won't show itself until it ripens. It is held in the soul for spans of time—especially painful splinters of the heart. It's quietly nourished there. Incremental teachings birth themselves from this soulful holding, and then are lived. People are deep mysteries, our lives a precious journey, sometimes outward into the world of experience— this world of beautiful, painful, terrifying form—but then also back to the deep interior of ourselves.

I can't know you more, Mama, and yet I feel as if I do, because I know myself a bit more. At times I feel the deeper you; not the one who could barely love, but the one who was wholly born from love and has returned to it; who is now part of the loving holding of the Feminine. She's the same one who mothered me barely enough, but who, along with my father, brought me to this place, where red rock country and native cultures nurtured me further. I wish we could have spoken of these things when you were alive. And yet, in your dying hours, I feel as though we did.

I send your teachings back now, those named and those that can't yet be named. I release them as blessings for you on the wings of Raven, Mama, flying high and free, knowing Raven can find you, wherever you are, and I cannot.

CHAPTER 39

Night Chant

It Is Finished In Beauty.
~ Navajo Blessing Way

Home now, in my own bed, back from the trip to your hometown where you were everywhere inside my eyes in thought, and in front of them in childhood memory. I unpack my suitcase and turn down the welcoming blankets on my bed. Climbing in, I shut off the dim light on the nightstand. Resting gratefully, I give myself to the twilight of sleep, but you've followed me beyond there, too, into the nightfall of dreamtime.

I dream of you and me and red rocks and blue sky

and water.

~

I am flying on a dream plane and am the dream plane, floating low and slow through an indigo sky, sitting outside on the wing, in nothingness, as the plane that I am takes me along sheer walls of red rock cliffs on the banks of the waters I love where I was once young.

~

I am the rocks and the lake and the love.

The sheer red dreamtime sandstone has waterfalls everywhere, water cascading down, through sandstone eyes that melt into hearing, and I am all thrill and fright in my everywhereness self that dreams and greater consciousness allow.

~

Far down below are small pink sand beaches at the edge of cliffs, feeling familiar and strange. I'm moving slowly along the edge, almost touching immense, tall cliffs

with water pouring over them everywhere, so much water,
water of pure love, songs of desert life water, spilling down
to narrow sandy beaches singing waves with joy.

~

I know in that dreamlike way of knowing that I'm
moving along narrow gorge canyons, all substance of my
life, these loving red rocks, red rocks shining inside me,
around me above and below, dreaming and being them
everywhere I go, blessing me all my life, no matter where I
am in time or place or country, no matter the good or bad
moment of my life, their living voice a steady beacon to
show me both my true home and the way I need go.

~

Now heading up the gorge that holds the sacred
rainbow stone arch, the living stone rainbow, protector
to those people here from the beginning of it all, of all the
realms of worlds, and for me too, radiating for everyone,
flying along as myself, as the dream plane, vibrant cliffs
alive with the waterfalls and red rocks and blue sky and
water that dissolve together, singing, and in dissolving
become magnificence.

~

Moving slowly, and slowly, and slowly; fear,
exhilaration and beauty move through seeing, breathing life
as a moving prayer, in the dreaming world of colors sung
alive, and yet beyond words that can name all colors.

~

I move through the glittering blue sky world toward
the sacred stone arch, knowing that when I reach that
sacred place, where the red canyon widens and the rainbow
sandstone arch lies hidden then is awakened in grace and
rises alive and is seeing and seen, the shining spirit pathway
will unfurl and you will be there, waiting for me, as I feel
you here already, just as you feel me coming to you as you
are free already, and I am free in dreamtime.

~

I fly on,
toward you and to the pathway landing,
where you and I will rise together,
where you wait for me in love, and as I pause there,
I awaken.

~

Benediction

"May it be beautiful before you

May it be beautiful behind you

May it be beautiful above you

May it be beautiful below you

May you walk in beauty, Mama

May you walk in beauty

May you walk in beauty."

~ Navajo Blessing Way

~

EPILOGUE: SPRING 2024

I sat on the bare dirt, looking closely at the small green shoots in my hand. They had tiny, fragrant bell-shaped white flowers atop them. The flowers ran up the shoot, and the ones at the top had yet to open. I turned it around, looking under the delicate bells. Their spicy perfume drifted out onto the air. I breathed it in slowly, closing my eyes. I opened them and turned, hearing the creaking of the backyard gate. A figure strode across the yard toward me. I held up my tiny shoot toward her.

"Look, they've started blooming. My Lily of the Valley flowers."

"Are those the ones from Indiana?"

"Yeah, this whole patch is. They were in a pot in New Mexico. I moved that same pot up here, and they stayed in it for another decade. It didn't seem like they wanted out until I moved here, into the woods. Then they wanted to be planted, so I put 'em in the ground."

"Oh, I remember that! Whose house did they come from again?"

"They're from your Great Grandma F's house," I said. "My Aunt Margie dug a bunch of them up after she died. She planted them in her own yard. I got mine by way of her." I picked another shoot, and handed it up to my daughter, who took it in her left hand, and brought it to her nose. She was left-handed, like Mama. "Isn't it lovely? They bloom around my birthday. Makes me think of Grandma F every year. There's so many! They've really gone wild since they were set free from that pot."

"Well...that's probably a good thing," my daughter said, looking away. "Because...I'm pretty sure the pot you gave me died."

"What? What happened?" I turned around to get a closer look at this girl whose pot of flowers had died.

"I just got super busy with work and the boys. I forgot to set them out in the rain, I guess, and they dried up. Then I watered them, probably too much, but nothing came back."

" Okay," I sighed. "Well, lucky for you, these special flowers aren't hard to come by. I've got bunches now. I'll dig more up, if you're sure yours are really dead."

"Yeah. They are. I'm sure." My daughter stood silently over me for a moment. "Thanks, Mom. They meant a lot to me. I didn't want to tell you, especially after Aunt Margie died last year. I'm so glad I got to go back with you and Aunt Sandi last time."

"Yeah, me, too. And I'm so glad you got to meet her. That meant so much to me. I know it took a lot of effort for you, but I really wanted you to see it all; the town, the German names, all the old places. And we saw the farmland! I hadn't been down there since I was a kid."

"It was amazing! It's so pretty there. I thought it was green here. I'd like to take the boys back there one day."

"I sure hope you do. And it's okay about the flowerpot," I added. "I'm pretty sure the ones Mama brought back didn't live, either," I said, grinning. "Let's go for that walk, if I can get off my knees."

"Want a hand up?"

"Sure, thanks." I held out my right hand, and my daughter took it in her left, and I slowly unfolded myself and stood up. I looked at my daughter, her long dark hair and bright smile, atop her ripped blue jeans and T-shirt. For a moment, she looked like Mama, in those early pictures of her, laughing, before she was married.

"Thanks, my dear," I said, letting go of her hand. "Let's head out! Do you mind just walking in the neighborhood?"

"No, I like it here." She looked back at me and paused. "I'm glad we live close by," she said, smiling.

~

Photographs

The four sisters. Clockwise from top left: Donna, Lynn, Blackie, the author and Sandi.

Mama and Daddy on leave from Navy;
St. Regis Hotel, NYC, circa 1944.

Resources for Further Reading

Abbey, Edward, *Desert Solitaire*, Touchstone, 1990

Abbey, Edward, *Fire On The Mountain*, Harper Perennial, 2012

Dickey, Sonia, *Sacrilege in Dinétah: Native Encounters with Glen Canyon Dam*, University of New Mexico dissertation, 8-19-2011

Geng, Gia-fu and English, Jane; *Lao Tsu: Tao Te Ching*, Vintage Books, 1974

Lee, Katie, *All My Rivers Are Gone*, Bower House, 1998

Nichols, Tad and Ladd, Gary, *Glen Canyon: Images of a Lost World*, Museum of New Mexico Press; First Edition (October 1, 1999)

Sjogren, Morgan, *Path of Light: A Walk Through Colliding Legacies of Glen Canyon*; Torrey House Press, 2022

Tempest Williams, Terry, *The Hour of Land: A Personal Topography of America's National Parks*; Picador, 2017

LINKS TO:

Adams, Mike, *A History of Glen Canyon and Page, Arizona*:
https://mikesdamphotojournal.com

Federal Indian Boarding School Initiative Investigative Report:
https://www.bia.gov/sites/default/files/dup/inline-files/bsi_investigative_report_may_2022_508.pdf

Lee's Ferry:
https://www.nps.gov/glca/learn/historyculture/leesferryhistory.htm

Navajo Blessing Way:
https://navajotraditionalteachings.com

Navajo Nation History:
https://www.navajo-nsn.gov/History

The Paria:
https://www.blm.gov/visit/paria-canyon-vermilion-cliffs-wilderness-area

Acknowledgments

The undertaking of writing a book is slow, long and solitary, and yet involves many people. A heartfelt thank you to my earliest readers: Anna-Lena, Gretchen, James, Linda G-B, Lynn, Sheri and Trish. You supported this new writer with your time, helpful feedback and enthusiasm.

Thank you to Sydney Weinberg, whose early assessment injected deep and broad feedback, allowing me to write a flowing storyline and create more space for you, the reader. I'm grateful to the Oregon Writer's Colony for the beautiful coastal writer's cabin, where I made good progress one very long weekend, spreading chapters across tables everywhere. To the exuberant librarian Heather and the Garden Home Gnomes, kudos for this writer-supportive library group where we entertain one another with our writing ideas, and hear from the most amazing writers (and one publisher) in Portland. And Rose Winter, your final editing and enthusiasm made the process smooth and easy.

And for you, Ms. Kali, my black cat so often with me in the writing studio, because you thought it was your apartment (and it was). You stayed sixteen years, and left after my final draft was finished. Thank you for your life with me. I miss you.

To the marvelous editor and writing coach Christi Krug, who worked with me in person before COVID, by Zoom after, then with all of us in her wonderfully soulful critique group. Christi, if you hadn't believed in my stories and writing, this book would not be here. Your belief was deep, firm and unwavering, and for that I am very grateful. And to the writers who passed through our critique group, especially Sue, Clay and Lola: your earnest listening and thoughtful feedback enriched me, and taught me more about the craft of writing, and about caring about writing. You are dear to me. May we meet again over the page.

And to my husband, the Green Man, who listened and supported me for years, through writing aches and pains, long rewrites, annoying time schedules, including solo breaks away exploring desert and red rock country. I am grateful for the breadth our life holds, and the way you keep the home fires burning. Thank you.

The wisdom of many dharma teachings, ancient and modernized, have upended and deepened my life. Advaita Vedanta—often considered the crown jewel of Indian thought—along with Tantra, have been transformative, as have teachers in those lineages. In current times, I am grateful to Rupert Spira, whose direct path has been a priceless sanctuary. I want to especially thank Saniel Bonder, whose Waking Down in Mutuality and related teachings brought the luminous heart of ancient tantric dharma into present day life. It gave me the impetus and sustenance needed to write this book. And a hug to Linda-Groves Bonder, who helped steady me, repeatedly, when I most needed it. As you would say, Linda, "Brava!"

To the Southern Paiute and Hopi tribal cultures, especially the Navajo People, or Diné, who possess an ancient physical and mystical bond with the homeland known to them as Dinétah. May all tribes flourish in their rights of self-determination, with permanent federal protections for sacred areas and meaningful, adequate water rights. May the Southern Paiute tribe, at last, receive a designated homeland.

Writing This Book

It feels essential to share how this book came about. I was visiting an old friend in Santa Fe several years ago. We had worked together at the legislature. While at her house, I underwent a transformation. Blocked for years from writing except in my own journals, I'd grown internally hardened, certain I'd be unable to achieve a dream I'd had since my twenties. One evening, her husband casually remarked that his latest book was taking longer to publish than he thought it would, but that this wasn't a problem. Hearing this, something came loose inside of me and let go, throughout my whole body. This letting go arose independently of any effort or thought, and continued in the same manner for two days. After that time, whatever energy had hardened inside me had dissolved, and an easy calm and inner sense of 'okayness' permeated me. Within a month of returning home, I sat down and began writing. Stories flowed easily as my child–self spoke through me, often directly to the spirit of my mother. These stories took years to rewrite, as I had little literary skill. Eventually, the contents settled into this book.

Wilderness Tithing*

    As a child who watched the filling of Glen Canyon, I feel compelled to support the preservation of the area in the ways that I can. The following organizations are nonprofits whose work helps these efforts. You can also help by making small donations, writing public comments on proposals affecting the area, and by respectfully exploring the exquisite landscape of the Colorado Plateau.

- Glen Canyon Institute

- Glen Canyon Conservancy

- Bears Ears Inter-Tribal Coalition

- Grand Staircase Escalante Partners

- National Park Trust

- Regulations.gov

    This wonderful term was coined by Ginger Harmon, co-founder of the women's wilderness advocacy nonprofit, Great Old Broads for Wilderness.

www.ingramcontent.com/pod-product-compliance
Lightning Source LLC
Chambersburg PA
CBHW021710120626
46545CB00004B/1486